The Pursuit of Porsha

How I Grew Into My Power and Purpose

PORSHA WILLIAMS

WORTHY
PUBLISHING

New York • Nashville

Worthy
Hachette Book Group
1290 Avenue of the Americas, New York, NY 10104
worthypublishing.com
twitter.com/WorthyPub

Originally published in hardcover and ebook by Worthy in November 2021
First Trade Paperback Edition: September 2022

Worthy is a division of Hachette Book Group, Inc. The Worthy name and logo are trademarks of Hachette Book Group, Inc.

The publisher is not responsible for websites (or their content) that are not owned by the publisher.

Library of Congress Cataloging-in-Publication Data
Names: Williams, Porsha, author.
Title: The pursuit of Porsha : how I grew into my power and purpose / Porsha Williams.
Description: Nashville : Worthy, 2021.
Identifiers: LCCN 2021023041 | ISBN 9781546015901 (hardcover) | ISBN 9781546015932 (ebook)
Subjects: LCSH: Williams, Porsha. | Television personalities—United States—Biography. | African American television personalities—Biography. | Actors—United States— Biography. | African American actors—Biography. | LCGFT: Autobiographies.
Classification: LCC PN1992.4.W555 A3 2021 | DDC 791.4502/8092 [B]—dc23
LC record available at https://lccn.loc.gov/2021023041

ISBN: 9781546015901 (hardcover), 9781546015932 (ebook), 9781546015925 (trade paperback)

Printed in the United States of America

LSC-C

Printing 1, 2022

To my lifesaver PJ,
Mommy's tears will never be your fears.
Love you forever!

CONTENTS

A NOTE FROM THE AUTHOR

To protect the privacy of my loved ones, and other people whom I've met and would rather forget, some names have been changed. Others have been erased.

INTRODUCTION

If you thought you knew my life after watching me on reality TV, get in and buckle your seat belt, because it's about to get really real.

After starring season after season on *The Real Housewives of Atlanta*, I felt there was still so much I never got a chance to say in those confessionals or never got to express at the reunions between throwing shade and receipts. So I've opened up my life here, page by page, to share my truth, my strength, and my pursuit of the real Porsha.

Some of what I'm about to share will be tough to hear. It was even tougher to write; that's why it took me years to do it. Although I knew God wanted me to bring voice to my story and my testimony, I avoided writing a book for a long time because any good book is your truth on paper. It's laying yourself bare and having to face yourself, your failures, and even your fears.

But the way I have been blessed, I believe it is my duty to tell these stories as a testimony for other young girls and women. I went from being homeless while starring on *The Real Housewives* to owning two successful businesses. Not to mention, I'm co-hosting the nationally syndicated talk show *Dish Nation* and Bravo's new late-night talk show *Chat Room* while also making headway into scripted television.

If there is one person I can touch with my story or save from making the same mistakes I did, then it was all worth it. Honestly, it was all worth it anyway because it made me the woman, the mother, the daughter, and the friend that I am today.

Every sparkling diamond has been put under pressure. I am no exception. Some of that pressure you've seen on television, but other moments you have no idea about—until now.

Sometimes when you watch someone on TV, you think you know her. But the woman you've seen on the show is only a small piece of me—a character at times. Even this book is a small piece of my blessing-filled life, but I hope that after laughing and crying with me, you understand the fullness of Porsha and how I became the proud Black woman I am today.

I've faced depression, heartache, and pain, and I've used joy, happiness, and my unwavering faith to get me through.

Thank you for loving and supporting me on this journey called life.

You ready?

CHAPTER ONE

"Hiiiii, welcome to Porsha's World!" I said cheerily while staring into a black camcorder.

At twelve years old, I already knew there was something to discover through that lens that didn't seem attainable in the confines of my childhood bedroom. My reality felt extraordinary through that lens.

During pre-production for my faux Home Shopping Network show, I had walked around my mother's house on Cameron Close, about thirty minutes outside of Decatur, Georgia, carefully examining and hand-selecting the items I deemed worthy to be sold later to my millions of fictional viewers. While I sat in my chair for my first-ever series, my mother's beautiful items, perched on different shelves, shone behind me while my dolls and stuffed animals served as my studio audience.

"We have this beautiful candle," I said, picking up my momma's smell goods while wearing the shoulder-padded jacket I'd swiped from her closet earlier. "We only have a hundred left! Oh my God, hurry up and buy them!"

At the time, I was living with my mom, whom everyone else called Ms. Diane, during the week and visiting my dad, Hosea, on the weekends. My parents had split by the time I was two or three years old. In my room, though, with its bay windows and vaulted ceilings, I felt like I had created my own safe haven.

It felt like the only space where I could dream a little bit bigger than those white walls. It felt like the only place where I felt comfortable to ask for more of myself and see more for myself, rather than the flat-chested, skinny, big-eyed stick—hateful words I had heard the other kids call me at school that I somehow believed to be true. I wanted to be more than the girl other kids called ugly. The one they called lame.

At that time, I could've never imagined some two decades later, millions would be watching me through similar black lenses, falling in love with me through my triumphs, my heartbreaks, my mistakes, and my overcome.

Back then, my twelve-year-old self found no relief at Chapel Hill Middle School in Decatur. I don't remember much about middle school, and it's probably because I didn't care much about it. I didn't really excel there because I didn't really pay attention. I just wanted to get through the day so I could run back to my room and be by myself. I used to sit there in my classroom staring out the windows, waiting to go home and return to my safe haven.

While other kids hung out with one another, played sports, or tore up the playground, I spent a lot of time in my room. I'd even tie a scarf around the doorknob just to be sure no one would unexpectedly come in and ruin my introverted fun. It would be full-blown bliss. Once I turned on that Jodeci from my pile of CDs, slow love songs would fill up any emptiness in my room…oh, you couldn't tell me nothing. I wasn't in love with anyone then, but *babyyyy* did I love to sing a good sad love song to pass the time.

When I wasn't chilling in my bedroom, I was running around with my older brother, Hosea, who was named after my dad and his dad. Believe it or not, I was a tomboy who wanted to run around the neighborhood until the streetlights came on instead of playing inside with dolls.

Hosea was only two years older than me but instead of that natural sibling rivalry, I was obsessed with my big brother. Our entire family was. At my momma's house, Hosea was her most cherished son, and at my father's house, he seemed to rule over everything. There was something about Hosea—he had this ability to be exactly who he was every second of the day. I was not only enamored with him, but also inspired by him.

When I wasn't loving on him, I was pranking him. We were always trading pranks on each other throughout our childhood because we were so close in age. He was always messing with me and I was always messing with him. And what was so frustrating was that everyone thought I was picking on him, but it was really the other way around.

Between pranks and getting in trouble for those pranks, we would explore our neighborhood in Ellenwood, Georgia, so much that we often heard as we zoomed by, "There go those Williams kids!"

Still, no one knew my secret pain.

No one has ever known of the deep sadness that seems to linger in the air around me because on the outside, I act completely opposite to how I'm feeling, by choice or for survival. At times even I can't tell. People think my life is so popping; that I always have people to talk to and always have friends to turn to. But that's not ever been my case. Ever.

Even though I considered her my best friend, I couldn't tell my mom all the thoughts running through my head. I couldn't tell my mom that I had held a bottle of pills, thinking about swallowing all of them, but deciding against it because I feared I'd be brain dead and I definitely didn't want to be that.

I couldn't tell her that I had tied a purple, red, and black scarf around my neck to see what it felt like to not live anymore, or that I had gone a step forward and tied that same colorful scarf to the door. I'm not sure what she'd think if I ever told her my body dropped to the ground—in surrender or relief? I'm still not sure.

What I was sure of, however, was just how hard my mom worked to ensure I had a certain lifestyle. She was my best friend. She is my best friend. She was a boss, having owned a daycare and learning centers in Atlanta, Georgia, educating hundreds of children.

Because I knew she was doing all she could to provide for me and my brother, I wasn't going to tell her about the bullying in school, and I definitely wasn't going to tell her about what I did in my room when no one was looking. The idea of disappointing my mom with this never-ending sadness felt like it could end my entire world. She was so busy. She didn't have time for this foolishness.

My whole existence felt like a disappointment and I didn't want to let her down one more time with a pathetic problem I couldn't explain. My unwavering depression made me feel so guilty, because I saw just how much my mom was sacrificing to give me every single thing I wanted out of life.

Even in middle school, I knew that suicide would be so selfish. I couldn't dare leave my mom when I loved her so much. I wouldn't want her to deal with that.

Thankfully, somehow mothers know, especially Black mothers. They seem to have a sixth sense about what their children are going through. (I understand that more and more with the birth of my own daughter, Pilar.) My mother, who was quick to discipline me but loved me beyond words, felt and knew what I didn't say; what I couldn't say while I struggled during middle school.

She offered me a lifeline.

"You and your brother are going to go talk to a friend of mine and I want you to just kind of tell them how you feel," my mom said casually one day while she was picking me up from school.

"How I feel about what?"

"Well, I can tell you more when we get there," she hinted. "Hosea is going, too, but I think it's important for you two to have someone to talk to—another friend."

But even this professionally trained stranger, perched in an office building that sat around the corner from a movie theater we always used to go to, couldn't heal my broken heart.

I visited this therapist twice before I decided that if anything, the entire exercise of sitting down and trying to explain what I was going through was stupid and a waste of time. If I couldn't understand what I was going through, how could I conceptualize it for someone else to analyze? I just didn't want to be asked all those piercing questions. I didn't have the answers. I couldn't pinpoint what issue could've been that bad for a twelve-year-old.

I mean, I hadn't even hit puberty yet. I hadn't gotten my period. Not only was I just coming into my womanhood, I was just coming into myself.

I did know, though, that even at my age, I was really good at pretending like I had it all together. It was the first time in my life that I had picked up that mask to hide how I truly felt.

So I never showed any emotion that might've seemed weak to my mom. I never, ever wanted her to think that I was sad. I never even wanted to cry in front of her because I wanted to protect her. I never wanted her to feel that she was the cause of it; that being a single mom made me somehow upset with life or upset with her. So I masked my sadness and my anger and my disappointments. Despite my frustrations, I held everything in.

I didn't realize that what I was feeling actually had a name and that I wasn't the only person suffering with depression. I wasn't even the only one suffering with depression in my family.

It wasn't until my divorce, decades later, that I was willing to confront it and when I did, I realized that I wasn't alone.

Just two weeks after my ex-husband, former NFL player Kordell Stewart, completely blindsided me by filing for divorce after only two years of marriage (don't worry, there's more on that later), I had to put on a brave face and fly to New York. Bravo, the network that airs *The*

Real Housewives of Atlanta, where I had just finished my first season, was holding its annual upfronts.

For those who don't know, television networks have what's called upfronts. They're these big, elaborate celebrity-filled parties, held every year, where the networks present their latest slate of programming, or shows, to lure advertisers into investing. Bravo had invited me, the housewife who had no house and was no longer a wife, to represent their highest-rated *Housewives* franchise at the time.

I didn't even think producers would want me back on the show as a newly single woman, so on one hand I was relieved when I got the call that I'd be joining my castmates Nene Leakes and Cynthia Bailey in New York to walk the party's bright-blue carpet. But on the other hand, it'd be the first time I'd be seen in public after the world learned I was getting divorced.

I had invested so much into my marriage—having given up my own business, as well as my friends and family, to be the perfect wife and stepmother. Now, just days after that life was ripped away from me, I had to talk to perfect strangers and the press, who would seize the opportunity to get a sound bite for their stories, not realizing that their questions were piercing daggers into my very broken heart.

It was a lot.

It became so hard to give evasive answers to journalists on the red—well, blue—carpet while trying to hold back tears that eventually the tears won and my willpower gave up. I ran to the bathroom inside the venue to let them fall freely, my younger sister Lauren there rubbing my back.

It wasn't until I had suffered through the party and took off my strapless kelly-green dress to hop on a Delta flight back home to Atlanta that everything hit me at once.

"What are you going to do?" Lauren asked me from her aisle seat in first class.

We were sipping on mimosas that the flight attendant had just placed between us while we made little families out of stretched-out Starbursts.

"I don't know," I said, staring out the tiny rounded plane window. "I have no idea. I'm just so sad. Am I supposed to feel this sad?"

Lauren didn't understand the question. So I elaborated.

"I just wish I could fix it," I said when she asked what I meant by that. "I thought I had it figured out. I had a husband, a stepson, and I thought I was going to have more kids.

"When you get married," I continued, "you're off the streets. You think this is it, but it wasn't. Clearly. I just can't believe this is happening. I set up my life to be Kordell's wife, to be a mom. I didn't set up my life to do anything after because there was no after. That was it."

The odd thing about it was, I wasn't even angry anymore. I wasn't even upset. I was beyond that. I was hopeless.

"Porsha, I know this seems like this is the worst thing that's ever happened to you in your life, but you'll get through this," Lauren said, breaking my train of thought.

"How do you know that?" I said, defiantly, not ready to receive advice.

"Because I've been there, where you're crying all day long, not understanding what's wrong with you," Lauren revealed for the first time to me.

I looked over at Lauren with new eyes while my little sister told me that while she was attending Spelman College, the all-girls historically Black institution in Atlanta, she had found a therapist to help her cope with what she had been feeling.

"I had been struggling with anxiety and I didn't have a name for it," Lauren admitted. "So I just felt stupid for feeling it."

"That's how I feel and I feel crazy for feeling this way."

"It's okay. You'll come out of it. You've been this way before and what happened? You came out of it. You're epic!" Lauren reminded me. "You're brave. You can get through anything."

My baby sister's words felt good hanging in the plane's thin air, but they failed to land. As much as I wanted to believe Lauren, it'd be weeks before I convinced myself that what I had put up with wasn't okay. It'd be months before I realized that I didn't have to endure emotional and physical abuse to have a family; that I didn't have to choose between success and love; that there was space in the world for both.

But thankfully, for the first time, I knew I wasn't alone in my mess. At least I knew that I wasn't the only one feeling helpless, and confused, and sad at times.

As I pushed around the sweet mushy families that lay on the plane's tray between my sister and I, Lauren would say something that would snap all my life's relationships into focus.

"You know," she said hesitantly, a painful moment that she didn't want to spill out obviously rolling around in her head. "My therapist said it all goes back to Dad."

CHAPTER TWO

I remember seeing Jesse Jackson kiss my sister's forehead, but Lauren didn't seem comforted. Instead, she looked super-annoyed.

She was only ten years old at the time, but I could tell she didn't want to stand up and shake hands any longer. She felt like I did. She wanted to get out of the church and mourn her father in peace—whatever mourning looked like at that age.

I was sixteen when my father died from a rare blood disease called paroxysmal nocturnal hemoglobinuria. To make a very complicated disease sound really simple, it's when the red blood cells don't act right.

My dad was only forty-three when he succumbed to the disease after an unsuccessful bone marrow transplant, but he had clearly already made a huge impact in the world. Just four days after his spirit left this world and my father officially became an ancestor, anybody who was connected to anybody who was connected to him seemed to gather inside Israel Baptist Church, which is located on a road in East Atlanta that's now called Hosea L. Williams Drive, named after his own father. Jesse, Dick Gregory, Mayor Bill Campbell, and every other important person in Atlanta, it seemed, was inside the brick church.

Although it was September, it was a rather cold day for Atlanta and before the service, I couldn't make myself move fast enough. Grief was weighing me down, bad, making my feet feel as if they were in quicksand. But instead of being worried that I'd be late to my own father's funeral, I felt nothing. Absolutely nothing. I had disconnected from the moment, surely to protect my heart. But I still managed to put on a silk black dress with a matching scarf that I kept tied around my neck that day to say my final goodbye to my father.

While the rest of my family—my father's six brothers and sisters along with their children—had gathered at my grandmother Juanita's house to ride in eight or so black limousines to take them to see my father for one last time, I strolled into the church late.

I walked past the throngs of people standing, sitting, and trying to cram comfortably into the sanctuary right to the front and sat down next to my mother. And although I saw so many faces I recognized—from school, from my mother's daycare, my dad's friends and my grandfather's inner circle—there were many other faces I couldn't place.

All I could remember was his casket, his final resting place. It was still open and atop the shiny box that would hold his life for all eternity were so many red roses. I just remember those red roses and how they cascaded down, filling up the church with a floral scent I just couldn't register.

"Hey! Can y'all close that now?"

It was Lauren's mother, Lisa, asking one of the church's trustees to finally close my dad's casket after it had been open for more than half the service. Even though I spent much of the funeral staring at the back of her head, I could tell Lauren was visibly upset about it. She even fell asleep for a little bit, probably not wanting to see her father that way anymore.

At my father's funeral, so many people wanted to memorialize him, including Dick Gregory, who thankfully made us all laugh by sharing anecdotes from my dad's life and remembering him for the hilarious, charismatic person he was.

My dad liked to say he was the average height of a Black man, which really meant he stood at five foot nine. My dad was like me in many ways. He was attractive, flashy, the type of guy who walked in a room and made you wonder, *Who is that?* Our family has really bad vision so he always had on a pair of glasses, the kind that turned dark in the sun. It always looked like he had on shades, but he pulled it off.

Dick spoke about Dad's great personality; the fact that he never walked through a room of strangers. He seemed to know all of Atlanta and all of Atlanta knew him.

I suppose he couldn't help it being raised by his father, the elder Hosea, who was Dr. Martin Luther King Jr.'s chief field lieutenant. My grandfather worked alongside Dr. King in their organization, the Southern Christian Leadership Conference, and later founded his own long-standing outreach, Hosea Feed the Hungry and Homeless.

His wife, my grandmother Juanita, was equally impressive, graduating third in her class from Savannah State College, eventually becoming a Georgia legislator and one of the first Black women to run for public office in the state.

When it came to his family, my dad was really warm, but when it came to his business, he was demanding and at times coldhearted. In fact, he loved to press buttons. He was the type where he could yell "Fuck you!" and hang up the phone and people would still say, "Hosea, you crazy but we love you for it."

Dad was a boss. He was a successful entrepreneur who owned a janitorial chemical supply company that sold cleaning supplies to major retailers like Home Depot. He got the idea from his father, who was a chemist. Before my grandfather became an iconic civil rights leader, he had earned his bachelor and master's degrees in chemistry from Morris Brown College and what's now known as Clark Atlanta University.

He was well respected for being fair and a truth teller, and if he didn't tell you the truth there was a good reason for it. He was very much a tell-you-like-it-is type of person and I admired that about him because he seemed to have a way with words and could make even bad situations feel good.

That was my dad.

The funeral seemed to drag on, but it ended with us having to shake everyone's hand at the end of service. We stood there exhausted from the memories, laughter, and tears, shaking each person's hand one by one as we tried to figure out what words to say in response to their *sorry for your loss*es and *condolences*. My replies never seemed to measure up to how I was feeling, as if I even knew what I was feeling. Looking back at the winding line of mourners inside the church, it felt like I would have to endure this uncomfortable back-and-forth for another twenty damn minutes.

I looked over at Lauren to see Aunt Jettie trying to pick her up, but her body looked like a limp doll in defiance. Clearly she wasn't cooperating; instead she dragged all her body weight to the floor. I don't remember running over to her, but I must've.

"Let's just get out of here," I told her, picking her ten-year-old body up with ease.

"I don't know how you knew you had to save me," Lauren whispered.

We found an empty limo waiting for us outside the gold-steepled church and climbed inside. I couldn't hold it in anymore. I never could have cried inside that church. I'm the type to never show that I'm upset even if I am, and I tried very hard to hide my hurt in front of the congregation. But inside the limo, watching the tears fall down Lauren's face, I couldn't help myself. I started crying, silent and stiff.

Lauren was crying, too, but as her big sister I felt like I needed to say something to fix this; to make us feel better even if I didn't believe the words coming out of my mouth just yet.

"It's going to be okay. He's in a better place," I mustered, which only made Lauren cry harder.

It was an oddly familiar moment because I was actually with Lauren inside Duke University Hospital the night my father passed away, September 21, 1998. It was more than a month after he had gotten a bone marrow transplant from his brother and he was recuperating, until he wasn't. He had developed graft-versus-host disease after his body rejected his brother's bone marrow.

It was that time of day when the nighttime blended into the morning. The time of day when usually the world is asleep, and the only people who are up have a problem to solve. My grandmother and aunts were holding one another's hands, surrounding my dad's bed in prayer. He was no longer conscious, but their faith persisted. In that familial amen corner, they spoke life into my dad, shared his hopes and dreams for this life, not realizing God already had a bigger plan for him.

This was lost on Lauren, who only knew it was bedtime. She couldn't stand up in that sterile room any longer with the machines forcing life into my dad, or at least trying to.

"I wanna lay downnnnnnn," she whined.

It was around 4:00 a.m. and honestly I wanted to lie down, too. So I took her out of Dad's hospital room in search of a nurse that could help. We found someone who opened a tiny room that was attached to Dad's room. There wasn't even enough space for us to lie down next to each other, so I ended up sleeping on the floor while Lauren lay slightly on top of me.

We were asleep when dawn turned to morning. We were asleep when Dad transitioned to the next life, but we were together. We heard the beeping—the machines keeping my dad alive—stop. We heard the nurses turn them all off, one by one.

By the time we walked back into my dad's room, the sterile space that was once filled with beeps and tones was now completely silent. Dad's body was still warm, but it was perfectly still for the first time.

Although I was only a teenager, my family thankfully let me see Dad's final transition with my own eyes. It didn't help me believe it any quicker; I still couldn't believe it was happening.

"He's still alive! He's still alive," I offered to my aunts in the room, who'd stood watch beside him as he made his way over.

"No, Porsha, he's not," one of my aunties corrected.

"He can't be…He can't be. It's not real. It's not real."

* * *

I don't remember my parents being in love, but I know that they were. I know that my brother was made in love. I know that I was made by love.

After they met at the University of Georgia—my mom was an undergrad while my dad was enrolled in their law school—they gravitated toward each other quickly and refused to let each other out of their orbit. I describe their falling in love like a celestial gravitational pull because if you knew my dad and got to know my mom, then you would understand the type of aura that I'm talking about. They both had the type of spirit where people were attracted to them. They both had it. Hell, my mom still has it. They were both attractive and charismatic and vivacious and outspoken. I guess we'd call it swag now.

By the time I had formed memories about what my early childhood was like, my mother had quit her job at my father's chemical company and thrown herself into being a housewife. A caretaker, a homemaker, a mother, and a wife were titles she was proud to hold and my mother showed me just how much joy and fulfillment could come from caring for your own family. She taught me that being a housewife was a worthy profession and that it took every God-given talent you had to care for your children and treat your man like the king he wanted to walk out in the world and become, all while keeping your own peace.

My dad, on the other hand, was very fun loving. I think it meant a lot to him to be The Fun Dad. He was also a very affectionate parent, so there was never a day when he wouldn't give me or my siblings hugs or kisses on the forehead.

Because I didn't live with him, there was this built-in absence and distance between us, so his touch meant a lot. It meant a lot to be wrapped up in his arms. It meant a lot to feel his love. It felt amazing to be the center of his joy while I had it. I cherished every single moment.

I remember one day in particular when he called me to plan a day date with just the two of us. My dad had four kids—two boys and two girls—so having one-on-one time with him was rare. On this day, the movie *Selena*, starring Jennifer Lopez, was coming out and he had called me to say that we were going to go see it together.

I couldn't wait. I was going to get a full day with my dad, just me and him? I would have him all to myself?! I could barely contain my excitement. My dad first took me to lunch, then we went to the movies to watch a fictionalized Selena sing her hit songs "Bidi Bidi Bom Bom" and the heart-wrenching ballad "I Could Fall in Love." As we watched her life play out, one that was cut short, I could hardly pay attention because I was too busy looking at my dad. I was just so happy to be there with him. On the drive home, we spoke about Selena and our favorite parts of the movie.

The day was so special to me that I even bought Selena's album, and to this day I'm the biggest fan of her music. I know all the words to every song and feel so warm when I hear her voice. It all takes me back to that day and how special it was to spend that time with him, getting to know him on a different level.

Because I was so young, I didn't realize my parents were having problems until my mother had reached the end of her understanding one day, yelling about something my young mind couldn't quite comprehend. Visibly upset, talking to herself about something my father shouldn't have done, she drove me right up to Dad's office inside the family company that he owned, with his employees poking their heads out of their offices to see what the commotion was all about, and left me square on his desk.

I wouldn't find out until I was much older that infidelity was the source of my mother's pain; a pain that I'd become too intimately familiar with in my own relationships decades later. Unfortunately, it wasn't just once or twice that my dad forgot his vows to my mom. It was the kind of disrespect that had my calm, understanding, gracious mother going full-on Bernadine from *Waiting to Exhale* and cutting up my dad's thousand-dollar suits.

By the time I was three years old, my parents had divorced. Unlike my mom, who would later throw herself into running a twenty-four-hour daycare center after their split, my dad spent his time running into the arms of another love of his life.

Dad met Lauren's mom, Lisa, a year after my parents' divorce. When you're that young, watching the man you love with your entire miniature heart give his love to someone other than your mom, it changes how you think about love and what you expect from it. It changes what you think is up and what you think is down, and suddenly life seems a bit more sideways.

I could tell my father not only still loved my mother, but respected her as well. Dad would always tell us how much of a good mom she was to us. It seemed they had a co-parenting relationship full of respect and maturity; I never heard either one of them speaking badly about the other.

He might've even feared her. I definitely had to make sure I was doing right, even while out of her sight, or we'd both get in trouble: "Don't tell your mom we're having pizza for dinner again. Make sure your homework is good because I don't want you going home telling your mom I didn't help you with it."

For her part, my mom just really wanted the best for my dad's next relationship so that I could grow up with stability and love and calm and tenderness. Mom always spoke highly about Dad's new wife and told me to be respectful of Lisa and listen to her. And after being a stepmom, I realized later on in life just how revolutionary it was for her to be so understanding of my dad and his new relationship.

Lisa wasn't a stepmom to me. She was more like a second mom. I mean, she basically helped raise me, especially since my father was insistent that we go over to their house every other weekend.

But well into my father's marriage to Lisa, whom I grew to love and admire, he began seeing his girlfriend. Because I was so young, I couldn't even begin to understand that if my father said he loved my mother, if he loved Lauren's mother, why would he need another woman?

Although I didn't understand it, it opened my young mind up to the possibility that this was okay—that a man having a wife and a girlfriend was what happened in marriages because my father did it. And not only did he do it, he didn't excuse it. It was a matter of fact. And he was still successful, he was still loved, and he was still highly regarded.

It didn't help that I saw my father's cheating with my own two bright eyes. He'd drag me on dates with his girlfriend around Atlanta, not hiding his indiscretions to his eldest daughter. Unknowingly, he created a confusing path forward for every single romantic relationship I'd have, where lies and secrets and cheating felt so common they were inconsequential.

I had to keep my father's secrets. It was a burden I didn't want and definitely didn't deserve. By watching his moves and listening to the words my father didn't say, I learned what it meant to lie to the ones you loved at a young age. And I learned the consequences when I dared to tell the truth.

I remember there was one time I was with my father when he went to his girlfriend's apartment. I was around ten years old and I didn't realize the rules of running around. I didn't know that you could see things that weren't supposed to be repeated. I mean, I was raised in a household where we told one another everything...or at least I thought we did.

Being slow to Dad's new rules, I had told Lisa what I had seen, which apparently I wasn't supposed to do. So on his next date with his girlfriend, instead of inviting me inside, my father made me wait in the car for hours, watching the sun burn its way across the sky at a snail's pace, my eyes following the sun below the horizon, hoping he'd come by the car to check on me or offer me reprieve inside. But no. He sat inside, with her. My little brother would periodically peek his head out of her apartment to check on me and make sure I was okay. My four-door purgatory was apparently my punishment for opening my mouth. It was my sentence for telling his truth.

It wasn't the only time Dad locked me away, which is a trigger I still carry with me to this day.

My father would lock me and my brothers in bathrooms, in bedrooms, the laundry room, and the basement when we were acting out or making too much noise as children. The doors were never actually locked, but we understood our punishment was that we could not leave. One by one, we were placed in separate rooms.

I don't think my dad meant any harm by it; it was just his way of putting us in a time-out. To him, it was better than spanking us. But being a naive dad, or an inexperienced dad, he would oftentimes forget about us. We would be in those rooms all day, and sometimes until nighttime.

Some days we'd create fun within the confines of our own imaginations while inside those four walls. Sometimes we'd even get to pick which room we wanted to go to, depending on the degree to which we had annoyed him.

But other days we longed to get out. It felt as if we made one mistake, we'd be sent away. What my dad likely thought was a convenient and less violent punishment ended up having its own repercussions.

When my mom would ask how our weekend at Dad's was, we hid

it. We lied about it. We dressed up our pain and then we detached from it.

This form of punishment birthed my need to be absolutely perfect. I became terrified of making any sort of mistake or not living up to the expectations men had for me, because I learned that if I did make a mistake, I could be left alone or locked up.

We constantly walked on eggshells. We never knew when he'd switch from The Fun Dad to The Strict Dad, from having water fights in the house and acting like a big brother to the whole house being on lockdown.

I didn't realize it then, but that punishment, which did seem like a normal punishment to me, contributed to the trauma and abandonment issues I'm still dealing with decades later.

We found ourselves lucky when we were locked in adjoined rooms. My little brother Brenton and I figured out a way to talk to each other through the vents, desperate to talk with someone or desperate to strategize how we'd get out. We'd often play "not it," trying to decide who would ask Daddy if we could come out of time-out.

One time I lost that game. I hesitantly opened my door—we knew not to open it until he said so—and had to go knock on Daddy's door. I really didn't want to, but it was better than staying one more second in a room by myself. I lightly knocked on the door. His voice boomed on the other side: "Come in!"

"Daddy…can we…come out now?" I said, scared of his reply.

"Ohhhh! Of course!" he said, completely softened and back to the loving, gracious, forgiving Daddy I knew. "Baby, come in here! I forgot y'all were in there, honestly. Go get your brothers. Tell them to come on in here."

And then he'd go back to being completely normal. So we followed his lead. We'd order pizza. We'd laugh, play games, watch the late show together. I was so used to forgiving what needed to be forgiven, moving on, pretending everything was fine.

I didn't understand, but I soon realized that if I wanted to be around him, I had to behave and keep my mouth shut.

Because he was so strict and protective over me, he didn't teach me anything about love and dating and men. He refused. Instead, he said what most fathers tell their teenage daughters: "Boys do not need to be on your mind right now. They don't want nothing but one thing, so keep away. You can't talk on the phone with boys and best believe, I'll kill any boy that comes in the house asking about you. Date when you're thirty-something."

When my father got sick, things changed. He was also raised in a blended family, and he felt it was really important that us kids stayed close no matter what. So my brother and I would spend every other weekend over at my dad's house in Stone Mountain, which was about thirty minutes away from my mom's house at that time. We'd run around with Lauren and my younger brother Brenton, who had a different mother. After he died, though, we stopped going over there. We never really got together anymore.

After my father's funeral, I didn't mourn. I couldn't fully mourn his death inside my mother's house, partly because I didn't want to hurt her feelings. I didn't want to mourn one parent in front of the other, if you know what I mean. And although my mom would always say, "It's okay. It's okay. He's your father," I still didn't want to show how devastated I was.

I sometimes felt like I didn't deserve to be sad because I was a teenager and I hadn't been spending as much time with him as I wanted to. There was school and boys and after-school activities and parties and The Mall. I could've been there more. I could've checked in on him more. I could've been a better daughter at the very moment he needed me to be, but instead I was a normal teenager who wanted to hang out with friends. So my guilt was misplaced. I felt like, how you gon' fall out and act like you can't handle losing your father when you didn't even go visit him last weekend?

My grief felt like a mask. I put eyeliner and powder and lipstick on my grief so that if any random person ever looked at me, they'd think I was okay. From the outside looking in, I probably seemed that way, but it still felt like a piece of me was missing. The worst part about my dad dying is that I knew that piece would never be recovered no matter how hard I searched for it. I'd always feel incomplete no matter what. At least that's what I thought back then.

When you're sixteen, grief has the uncanny ability to blur every bit of common sense you have, tainting every pure space in your heart and every real thought in your mind. So every time you feel, your mind wanders back—whether willingly or because of your guilt for trying to move on—to a deep longing for someone you know is not coming back.

As foreign as it was to me, grief also felt oddly familiar, almost like my own shadow, following me around as I lived my life. Oftentimes

I had no idea it was right there beside me, keeping me company. But as I continued to live my life and the sun shone brighter on me, even as I found its warmth and found life's joys, or laughed at a really good joke, or danced my cares away, it was still right there casting a shadow on that dark part of my heart, the part of my heart that refused to let go.

I knew my dad's death would have an effect on me, but I didn't realize how much it would impact me and for how long. I didn't realize that even at thirty-nine years old, I'd still be dealing with loving someone I've lost. I didn't expect that feeling of loss to show up again and again in relationships where it had no business popping in, where it didn't belong. With grief hanging on me like a stank I couldn't wash off, it seemed like a dog whistle, leading me to toxic relationships that would steal my joy.

Trying to love after you lose the sun in your universe—or perhaps he was the moon; either way he was a constant—is impossible. His death happened exactly at the moment when it felt like I needed him the most—in the years where I was going into dating and really graduating from being a girl and developing into a young woman.

I think about the memories that I can't make with my dad to this day; those moments I'll never have with him. When I turned seventeen, my first thought was about what he'd miss in the days of my life I had yet to live.

I thought about Dad not seeing me walk across the stage at my high school graduation. I thought about him not actually meeting a guy I liked because he never wanted me to date. But I just knew, he and I both knew, that one day I would meet someone and that guy would have to get my dad's approval before taking me out on a date. And my dad would barely let the dude in the house because he'd try to scare the crap out of him and make sure that nothing happened to his baby girl. I also thought about how he'd never get to walk me down the aisle or meet his grandkids.

I'd never have that protection because he was gone. As a young girl who was now alone in the world, I felt very insecure. I'd had a dad that I loved and revered, who protected me and wanted me to know right from wrong, and then all of a sudden I didn't.

I've learned to live happily with the blessing that life does indeed continue to ebb and flow, giving me more opportunities to make my dad proud. Every time I utter my own name, with his name attached to mine, I'm reminded of just how much I'm like him: able to walk into a room and hold its attention with my will, able to believe in myself enough to be entrepreneurial and create something out of nothing, and able to believe in the divine blessing of what it means to be Black, a lesson he passed down from his own father.

I am genuinely proud to be his girl, his daughter, a Williams. I'm proud to carry his legacy in my heart and in my stride.

While I came to terms with living without my dad, I was also thanking God that I had a praying mother, who not only taught me how to go to Jesus when I needed help, but also taught me how to be a boss.

CHAPTER THREE

For many women, becoming a housewife is a choice.

And becoming a housewife—a role not necessarily defined by a woman's partnership with her husband, but by her finding fulfillment in serving her family and her community—was definitely a choice I made.

Let's be clear: I'm not talking about the women, or caricatures of women, that you've seen on the show that I've helped make successful. We all know that's a cute catchy title that barely scratches the surface of what being a housewife is in reality.

Before cameras started rolling a year into my marriage to Kordell, I chose to be a housewife—to love and care for my family, to run a household, manage a household and take care of the household. I embraced all the tenets of how a traditional housewife was defined: You take care of your man, who sets the vision for the household.

You take care of the children to ensure they're loved, protected, and comforted. In return, you not only have support and peace of mind, but you also have love.

No matter what people have chosen to believe after watching my first season of *Housewives*, being a housewife off-screen was a persona I was still getting used to. I hadn't mastered it yet.

I was raised to be a boss.

Having been raised by an entrepreneur who owned successful daycare franchises in the Atlanta area, I saw firsthand the definition of hustle. I saw up close how hustle felt, how hustle moved, and how hustle got back up after being knocked down by unforeseen circumstances and people. Whether it was by observation or through osmosis, I got it from my mother.

I mean, she was the type of hustler who ran a twenty-four-hour daycare right after she divorced my father. When she needed to, she even brought in a cot for me to sleep on while she took care of the community.

Although my mother was a single mom, her only limitation seemed to be time—not having enough of it to spread out between running her daycare center and taking care of me and my brother. My mother was the type of woman that when she saw something she wanted, she would just get it. If there was something she wanted to do, she just did it. The fact that she didn't have a husband to run ideas by only seemed—to me—to be a benefit, not a detriment.

In fact, I was raised by two entrepreneurs. As you know, my dad also owned his own company. So I understood very early on the power of ownership—whether that was owning your own business or owning your own story. I knew I had what it took to bet on myself and materialize wealth that benefited not just myself but my community. That's a tool I'd have to keep taking out of my toolbox and sharpening throughout my life.

If you let my mom tell it, her daycares were true learning centers that offered everything from classes on parenting to workshops on how to dress for a job interview.

We'd go knocking on doors in Carver Homes and Capital City, passing out flyers to promote the daycare center. After we got families to believe in what we were doing, we'd often drive them thirty minutes to our plush, newly redesigned facility to ensure they got there safely. We'd go above and beyond because it felt like our duty to not only take care of these children, but put them in a position to excel. Oftentimes, we'd be taking care of families with four or five children who might not have been eating well at home. But at our daycare, they'd eat two meals plus snacks. We'd even put some of the children in sinks to bathe them because their young parents needed an extra hand.

The families were so grateful, and so were we because we knew how important it was to care for the children in our community. There was a need and we met it. If she could've cloned herself, my mother probably would've opened up more centers, because caregiving fed her in a way that other businesses couldn't have.

Our daycare served a very maternal need for my mother, who grew up in Asbury Park, New Jersey. Even when she was a child, she was always caring for other children in her neighborhood—watching them and making a special afternoon snack for them. Just like I grew up staring into the dark end of a camcorder, my mother grew up caring for children. That's the only job she ever had before moving to Atlanta in the ninth grade. Being raised by a family of preachers and teachers, my mother loved giving back in this way—another extension of my family's legacy of service to the Atlanta community.

My mother loved having me help out at the daycare center. It was another chance for us to bond and spend time with each other while providing for our own family. I didn't treat it as an afternoon job, or like I was just helping my mom out. I truly felt like this was my business—because in essence it was. I was seventeen, but I would take off my little-girl hat and put on my boss-woman hat when I walked through that threshold.

My mom would tell me, "Miss Jessica needs to be fired because she's been late and we just can't take it anymore. So you're gonna need to fire her."

"Meeee?!"

With my mom's help, I quickly learned how to handle these delicate conversations. Our company—and its employees—were important to us, and that meant we wanted them to learn and grow from their mistakes, not just send them on their way.

When I let people go, I didn't just say, "You're fired. Now get going." I really wanted to emphasize that they were only fired because we valued them and they had disappointed us.

Your staff is only as good as its training, and my mom and I were invested in investing in people even when they didn't meet our expectations and no longer met our needs. I always wanted to encourage people, even in one of their darkest moments, that although this opportunity wasn't here for them anymore, I still wanted them to do better in the future.

But I'll admit, when I wasn't about my business, it was hard not to slip back into my seventeen-year-old ways. Who wouldn't?

My mom, brother, and I had just moved into this gorgeous house in a Stone Mountain cul-de-sac. After days spent at school where I focused on graduating so I could run my own daycare, and afternoons working alongside my mom at her daycare, I spent my nights taking full advantage of finally filling out.

If I was made fun of by boys in middle school for being flat chested and having big eyes, those same boys were falling over themselves now to ride around Atlanta with my filled-out chest and eyes that were described as dreamy. It's funny how your worst qualities become the things that make you desirable.

So on this particular day, my girls and I skipped the last couple of classes at school and piled into a teeny-tiny car to ride around town with some boys. The car was so small, and with so many of us trying to squeeze in, the only way we could all make it safely was if we sat on the boys' laps. It's not like we minded…we definitely didn't.

Nestled on top of my guy, another suggested we spark up. It was only my second time smoking weed, but magically, a perfectly rolled blunt appeared and soon our car turned into a hot box.

We were smoking, and laughing, and smoking, and giggling, and smoking, and kissing. It was the perfect teenage afternoon when you didn't have to worry about responsibilities at the family business. I could just be a teenager for once.

We rode around a bit until we made our way back to my driveway because I thought my mom wasn't home—she was one of those moms that went to work early and came home late. But pulling up to my house, it looked as if she might be home after all. We just weren't really sure.

It felt like we zoomed past the house to check, but apparently in our haze we drove by realllllly, reallllllly slowly. That's when I finally spotted her car.

"Y'all! Y'all! Put that out, that's my mom's car," I told the boys.

We didn't even want to roll down the window for fear that the smell of marijuana would cascade out the car window and completely tell on us. But we didn't know what to do. I know I didn't, especially since I was already high as the top of Stone Mountain.

We tried to ease the car down the cul-de-sac, hoping she wouldn't see us creeping past her driveway. But that of course didn't work, seeing as there's only one way into our street and one way out. Next thing I knew my momma was out of the house and running up to our teeny-tiny car, saying something I couldn't make out.

"Porsha! Porsha! Is that your little ass in there?" I thought I heard her say through my green haze.

I didn't even want to answer her. I just hoped I was sober enough to string words together that made sense. (Spoiler: I wasn't.) My mom came to my side of the car, saw me sitting on a boy's lap, and practically snatched me through the car window and dragged me back into the house. Before she closed the door, though, she had some final words for my friends:

"Y'all, get out my driveway! Go home!"

I was too high to even be embarrassed.

I never really tried my mom because I knew she could get me together real quick if I ever did, and tonight she was proving me right. Thankfully, before she started her you're-in-trouble speech, she told me to sit down and handed me a glass of water. I desperately needed water in this moment because I could barely focus on what was going on; at least I couldn't without breaking out in giggles.

"Porsha, I'm not upset with you."

"You're not?" I looked at my mom like she was crazy, but I definitely wasn't going to argue with her.

"No, I'm not. I'm not upset that you're smoking reefer..."

When the word *reefer* came out of my mother's mouth, I couldn't help crack a smile. I tried to hold it together so I wouldn't break out into a full belly laugh. Seriously, why was she trying to have this conversation with me high? Why?

"You're high. You're high," she said at the sight of me trying to hold back a laugh. "There's no point in even screaming at you right now."

With my mother's voice coming back into focus, I heard her say, "I'm more upset that you would do it in public. We live in this neighborhood. We live in Stone Mountain with these racist white people. So they're already looking for something wrong and you're sitting up there in a car, driving around and smoking reefer. It's not smart, Porsha. It's not smart. You could have an accident. And your friends aren't even looking out for you because if they were looking out for you, they would've known better."

I couldn't help but tune out from her well-meaning diatribe. I was still high and serious words just refused to land. What did she expect?

"The next time someone offers you some reefer, you don't have to take it. Say you had some last week and it gave you a bad headache or something. Just be smart. You have a lot to lose."

My mother was right. I was months away from graduating from Open Campus, a specialized high school in Atlanta. Since my parents ran their own businesses, college was never a necessity, so I was footsteps away from being my own boss.

After graduation, I ran full speed ahead into creating the life that I saw for myself and I had no one telling me I couldn't be anything I wanted to be. I just had to figure out what that was first.

Before I opened my own daycare, a dream that would come into fruition when I was just twenty-four years old, I did my fair share of odd jobs just like any other twenty-something who had dreams of being more than what she saw around her.

I sold furniture and truth be told, I was the number one saleswoman on that floor. I did a bit of modeling. I even became "a video girl." And no, not like a video hoe or anything like that. I was more like a pretty face casting directors would book for music videos to dance beside, sit beside, or fake-laugh beside whatever rapper was putting B-roll to his songs at that moment. In Atlanta, home of So So Def Recordings and Disturbing Tha Peace, there was plenty of opportunity.

In my early twenties, I was on the set of a music video for 8Ball & MJG. Don't ask me to tell you what song it was for because I don't remember. What I do remember is that on the set of that video shoot, I'd meet a man who'd force me to learn the power of choosing myself. While it was a lesson I'd have to continue to learn over and

THE PURSUIT OF PORSHA

over and over again throughout my life, the first time is always the hardest.

I had just finished getting my hair and makeup done on set—that's back when they had budgets for glam—and I was sitting near craft services, where the crew had set up lunch with a variety of snacks. I grabbed my food and sat down at a table by myself away from the crowd. I didn't mind sitting and eating by myself until it was time to do my part for the music video. It was better than looking thirsty or competing with the other girls who were all up in the artists' faces, trying to get a look or a moment or a number or whatever they wanted.

I don't judge; it's just that I didn't need any of that. I didn't want any of that. I just wanted something more for myself. I wanted to make a name for myself. I didn't know how to get there, but I knew being back in front of that tiny black lens, the one I found comfort staring into in my childhood bedroom, could definitely help. So here I was, eating and waiting for my name to be called.

"Why you over here sitting by yourself?"

I looked up and didn't see the casting director or production assistant I was expecting to see. Instead, it was this tall, handsome man with kind eyes and a really thick neck.

"Well," I said, looking up and deciding to answer him honestly, "because I'm here working and I don't talk to people while I'm on set. So whatever it is you're about to say, I'm not interested."

"Wordddd?" he replied. A broad smile couldn't help but spread itself across his chocolate-brown face. The way he was smiling at me made me almost regret my stupid "on set" rule.

"No, I don't talk to people when I'm on set," I repeated, moving my eyes reluctantly back down to my plate of food.

Unnerved, he sat down anyway. We ate in silence until he finally gave up on the idea, realizing I was dead serious. I didn't see him on set for the rest of the day. It didn't stop him from giving a production assistant a piece of paper with his name and number on it to pass on to me. You can't hate a man for trying.

I reluctantly texted Clinton Portis a few days later and we began a years-long on-again, off-again relationship that eventually forced me to advocate for who I was and who I was becoming: this woman I was in pursuit of. A woman who didn't need to think of herself as royalty to believe she was worthy. A woman who treasured the desires of her heart, even if they were never whispered aloud because they carried in their unspoken words a destiny yet to be fulfilled. A woman whose measured step was filled with purpose and light and laughter.

Back when I met Clinton, I didn't know this woman yet, but I was about to find her.

When we eventually started talking on the phone, I realized that he didn't even live in Atlanta. I had no clue who he was and what he did. I would later learn he was the star running back for what's now known as the Washington Football Team (but back then was called the Washington Redskins—a name no one liked because of how obviously racist it was).

He never spoke about football, though. For months, we spoke about everything but football. He told me he was born in Mississippi and grew up in Florida. He spoke about his family a lot, which endeared him to me because I love my family, too. And he was clearly a momma's boy because he always mentioned her, which made me fall for him even more.

It wasn't until he invited me out to his home, which was outside DC, that I realized what he did for a living. He opened his garage and I saw his jerseys, sitting inside frames, hanging up on the walls. The numbers 28 and 26 stared back at me.

"Wait, who are you?" I asked him.

Back then, I never thought to google a person's name. It's just not something me and my girls did back then.

"That's what I like about you," Clinton said, not answering my question. "You didn't know who I was when we met so I knew you didn't like me for my money."

After that trip, Clinton would fly me to the DMV—the Washington, DC, Maryland, and Virginia area—a lot. And when I wasn't flying there, he'd come down to Atlanta to see me. He came down so much to see me that he eventually got a place down here.

During football season, it seemed like the requests were nonstop. "Come see me. Come watch my game," he'd say, and I didn't mind because in my twenties Clinton was opening me up to a different world I didn't know existed. Because he'd always want me to fly and meet him, I'd come up with some creative excuses to get out of work. At this time, I was still selling furniture and I would walk into work ready to get an Oscar for the performance I was about to give.

That morning, I wouldn't wear any makeup on my face because I normally have really dark circles under my eyes and I had to sell my sudden mystery illness. *Cough!* I'd try to walk around the store, fumbling about just a little bit before I eventually 'fessed up that I just didn't feel well—*cough!*—and I had come down with something.

My supervisors would be like, "Oooooh yeah, Porsha. You look really sick. Please, go home and take care of yourself."

And I'd definitely take care of myself, just not in the way they were thinking. I'd run out of that store, go straight home, pack my bag, and catch my flight that same day to go see Clinton.

Once I landed, I'd head to FedEx Field, the eighty-thousand-seat stadium in Prince Georges County, Maryland, where I'd have to mingle with the other football players' girlfriends and wives. Immediately I noticed the strangest thing: All the wives and girlfriends were white. I was the only Black girl staring back at them. On a team that had over fifty players, the majority of them being Black men, why was I the only non-mixed, brown-skinned Black girl there? It was weird. Plain and simple.

That's when I realized that football players wouldn't date us. They just wouldn't. It was strange because even in my early twenties I had been to enough parties in Atlanta to know that football players would party with us. They would kick it with us in the club. They would chill with us in the hotel. They would sleep with us. They would even buy us nice things to put a smile on our faces or keep our mouths shut.

But when it came to getting serious, or getting married, when it came to being inside that coveted stadium box, which earned you respect from the fellow girlfriends and wives, we wouldn't be there. They would marry the white girls. Even if a girl was mixed, she still stayed out of the sun and got blond streaks put in her hair to really blend in. I respected Clinton so much for being his own person and having me there to represent him. He was proud to be with a Black woman.

I was the only one who would show up as a Black woman, with my weave down to my butt and my baby hair popping on my forehead. It's sad, but I honestly think that's how I had an advantage. Because of my baby hair, I didn't look like a "regular Black girl"—whatever the hell that means. But I've heard it enough times from men that I've started to take their word at face value, even as it revealed just how devalued Black women are. Even though Black women come in so many different shades and hair textures and eye colors, somehow thanks to my swoops and a little bit of edge control, I looked more "exotic" and more palatable for that football player crowd.

When I'd walk through the stadium wearing Clinton's number on my back, it made me feel proud because Clinton had chosen a Black woman to represent him in his most sacred space—at work. But I couldn't help feeling a bit sad, too, that there were so many men born to Black women, raised by Black women, and cared for by Black women, who didn't see the beauty in us.

Sure, there was always the occasional player who genuinely fell in love with his bride. I'd never knock anyone for finding love, but when an entire team seemingly does it, it's obvious that marrying a white woman had become sort of a status symbol. To me it can't be anything but status because I know they love Black women. I've seen it with my own eyes.

Between flights back and forth from the DMV to Atlanta, I had grown tired of picking out couches, chairs, and side tables for my customers and decided it was time to start my own business.

I knew that I had to set a standard of excellence in whatever business I decided to launch. After all, I was following in the footsteps of my mother, my father, and my grandfather, who were all well known in Atlanta as smart and savvy businesspeople. If it had the Williams name on it, it had to not only set the standard, but exceed it. It had to be above average, and I was committed to seeing that through.

After my grandfather passed away, I used the inheritance money he had left me to invest in myself and invest in hundreds of children across Atlanta. My mother's training ground, Three Stages, prepared me to open my own daycare center. When I was twenty-four years old, I worked hard to create a safe space—ten thousand square feet to be exact—for two hundred families all across Atlanta.

Because I was so young you would think I'd be nervous about opening a facility that offered home pickup, drop-off, and twenty-four-hour care, just like my mother's center, which had been the first to ever offer a service like that. But I wasn't, because I knew the business like the back of my hand. I knew what to do to get it started. I knew you had to pick the right location, and the one I eventually chose was in desperate need of the type of care that we provided. I knew how to market—and we did it old school, going into the neighborhood from door to door to pass out flyers, just like my momma taught me—so I was confident that we were going to do well.

At the time, I didn't think it was a big deal to open my own business, because my brother and I were raised to do just that. But now looking back, I realize that every twenty-four-year-old ain't out there running their own business. They're just graduating from college, and figuring out what they want to do, and applying to different jobs. That's an amazing path, too, of course, but if it wasn't for my mother instilling such an A-level work ethic in me, watching her set a foundation for excellence for me as an entrepreneur, there's no way I would've had the courage and fortitude to run my own company at such an early age.

Thankfully, my mother would often remind me that it didn't matter what you did for a living, you just had to be the best at it and make sure you loved it. So I knew that running my daycare was something that I'd love and pour myself into.

A true entrepreneur is only in the business that they know is going to be successful. And to be honest, a true entrepreneur is a dreamer. Whatever problem they're solving, or issue they're fixing, or business they own, or business they're building, they have invested money, time, blood, sweat, and tears into it. They have to believe in it. Even on those dark days when everything seems to be going wrong and they can't pay the bills and they're robbing Peter to pay Paul, they have to remember their dream and have faith that they're in this position to be a blessing for a reason.

It takes your whole heart to be a boss. I didn't get days off. I was the janitor, the secretary, the marketing maven, the bookkeeper and accountant, the front-desk greeter, and the trainer. I couldn't say *I quit* if I had a hard week or somebody on my staff was getting on my nerves. I couldn't just not show up to work that day because there were hundreds of kids counting on me. So it didn't matter what type of day I was having—whether my man got on my nerves or my tire blew out—I had to find a way. Correction: I had to make a way.

For a lot of entrepreneurs, it's hard to step into the role of boss and shed that feeling that you're not supposed to be here, you're not supposed to own this, or you're not supposed to have this. It's also intimidating for a lot of people to say that they own businesses because that means they fully take on the responsibility of the business and have to deal with not only the successes of that business, but more important the failures—and the failures do come.

I remember there was one time that I couldn't make payroll. After my employees worked hard—from 9:00 a.m. to 5:00 p.m. taking care of beautiful Black children—I didn't have enough money for their paychecks.

Although I was leasing the building that housed my daycare, for some reason I was the one paying for plumbing and it just so happened that we started having water issues—thousands and thousands of dollars in water issues. Plus, I wanted to expand the building and give my children more room to run, jump, and play. But my income and my overhead weren't adding up. Despite having more than two hundred children under my care, I just didn't have it. I had failed. I had failed my dream and I had failed the people I relied on day in and day out.

I had to ask Clinton a couple of times to lend me money to make payroll. And he did it. He did it with no questions asked. He held me down and I'm thankful for that.

It wasn't long after that, between flying in and out of the DMV while running my own business, that I began to feel a bit worn out. I was so used to being constantly on the go, trying not to let anything stop me, that I didn't realize I wasn't getting nauseous from the altitude. I wasn't feeling fatigued from the trip. I was pregnant.

I called Clinton to tell him the happy news. I was so excited this was happening and, more important, that it was happening with him.

For as long as I could remember, I knew that my purpose was to be a mother. I knew that it was my destiny to cover a little, tiny human and protect them and guide them and comfort them and inspire them. I always felt that having a child would give me something even more to live for as I pushed past those darker moments that would occasionally creep into my bedroom at night when all the day's noise would cease.

I felt motherhood would save my life. So when I found out I was carrying Clinton's child, I felt like I had been thrown a life raft.

I imagined the news that I was pregnant would be met with excitement. But sadly, it wasn't. Instead it was met with shock, skepticism, disappointment, coldness, and reluctance. The words he shared hurt so badly that my memory has largely blocked them, for fear that they'd break my heart over and over again at the mere thought.

I couldn't believe it. I told him that, yes, I was having his baby.

"Okay. Fine, Porsha, if you're going to have the baby, then I want it."

"Excuse me? You want what?"

"I want the baby. After you give birth, give it to me and my mother. We'll raise the baby."

"What, Clinton? What are you even talking about? No!"

What I really wanted to say to him was, *Oh hell no!* I had already gone to the doctor to confirm I was pregnant. I was so happy to be having a baby and to be having his baby, I could barely hold in who my baby daddy was at doctors' visits. I was even foolishly telling the doctor that, "I'm pregnant by Clinton Portis." It was not because of who he was. It was never about who he was, but rather because I was happy to have motherhood. I was happy that he had, in some ways, gifted me that title I had longed for since I understood the depths of love my own mother showed me. I couldn't wait to pass on that generational blessing.

But it didn't take me long to realize that my vision was one-sided. Clinton didn't want to have a baby with me. He wanted to make love with me, but he didn't want to have a baby with me. Ironic.

As excited as I was, I wasn't going to try to convince him. My pride had its limits and they were already being tested. So I was forced to think about alternative visions for my future—ones that wouldn't involve him. The mere thought of that, of holding his child in my sacred space while thinking of cutting him out of my life forever, was unbearable.

At this point we had been off-and-on for a while, letting the years clock in behind us as we lived a carefree life. It wasn't a relationship that was supposed to lead here. This wasn't supposed to happen. But when it did, I opened my mind up to the possibility because of how much I loved him and how much I knew he loved me, but he just couldn't see it.

I thought about raising our child on my own and how I'd be bringing my child into a very broken situation. I thought about the type of mother that I would have to be to wake up every day with a smile on my face, ready to nurture, cook every meal, wash every bottle and every onesie, clean every dirty diaper and dirty nose, rock my baby to sleep every single night, with my back aching and my arms shaking because I just wanted a break from it all—and never being able to take one because I'd be all this child had.

I thought about the mother I'd have to be to pull that off in my twenties, or at any age really, carrying that load all by myself. It was unfathomable. Unthinkable. I know mothers do it every single day. Hell, my mom did it. And fathers do it every single day, too, but I just wasn't sure I could do it.

I thought about another road, too. One where I didn't have to do it alone.

After a lot of somber contemplation—without involving anyone else, including my mother who had gone with me to doctors' visits— I decided to have an abortion. For some reason, this decision felt really easy to make because I knew it would be in the best interest of my child.

Thankfully, my mother was supportive of my decision because she knew it wasn't an easy one to make—not by any means. She knew how much I longed to be a mother, and every good mother knows how to spot toxic and dangerous situations to protect their children, even those who are unborn.

Clinton had sold me a fairy tale that just didn't exist for us. It definitely didn't exist for me, and I was heartbroken. I honestly thought having a baby would bring us together. I thought he'd be happy to have his first child with me. I later found out that even his mother wasn't supportive of our situation, joking that she wanted to "take me to Maury" to determine if the child was really his.

Because I was always so desperately looking for his approval, I let him take something away from me that I cherished. I just couldn't fathom raising a child with a man who couldn't see my value as a mother. He wanted me to just hand over our child like he had ordered it off Amazon. I just…I honestly still can't believe it.

After he said those words, it was never the same.

CHAPTER FOUR

I met Southern Jon through my cousin Tip.

We had gone out somewhere, running around Atlanta, doing what you do when you're in your twenties, and we had bumped into him. It didn't take him long to leave with my number. I knew he had dated one of my cousin's friends, but I didn't realize just how deep it was between them; at the time, I just thought that we both saw him at the same time and after a night of flirting, he chose me. But after a month went by, my cousin called me up to clarify a few things.

"My friend is kinda mad at me because you're talking to him," Tip admitted.

"What do you mean? We met him at the same time...and he chose me. Tell her sorry," I spat back a little sarcastically.

"No, I guess I didn't realize that they had had a relationship before. I didn't really know they were that close...but she said he can be crazy."

"What do you mean crazyyyy," I said, wanting her to spell it out for me before abruptly changing my mind. "You know what? Whatever. It doesn't matter. He's amazing to me."

And he was. Southern Jon was like the quintessential guy from Ellenwood: a country boy. He was not bad looking, but he had scars from a serious car accident and a slight limp.

But I didn't care about any of that because he was a country boy and I felt in my heart that he could be my country husband and we could live happily ever after in the country.

Southern Jon owned several franchises and had bought a plot of land in South Carolina that all his family lived on. He had built a home for his mother, his aunts, and their kids, and he wanted to build himself his own home on that property so everyone could live in a makeshift village.

When you pulled up to the property, his aunties and nem were sitting out on the porch, watching the grass grow. The kids were playing outside. The dog was running around, barking at the wind. It really looked like a scene out of a picture book.

The idea of creating a village really appealed to me because it was how I wanted to raise my own family, surrounded by my mom and my sister and my brother. So to have a man who valued family the way I did was amazing to me. In my mind, based on how he treated his family, I thought we were equally yoked. Especially when I saw how he treated his grandmother.

Since Southern Jon would visit her all the time, it wasn't long before we were introduced. She was this really, really sweet lady who didn't move around much, and she didn't need to, especially since the loves of her life would show up to love on her. You could tell how familiar and close they were. You could tell Jon would make it a point to visit her and I just thought it was so sweet that a grown man, busy with his own life, would take the time to always visit his grandmother. To me it spoke to his character. And after dating a few city guys who seemed more concerned about getting money, it was refreshing to date a country boy.

Southern Jon rolled around in a big white Hummer. Sitting in the passenger seat with him, I felt so protected, and I craved that. I'm not sure if it was because I mourned the loss of my own protector at just sixteen years old and I was sort of looking for somebody to guide me, but I felt so comfortable riding shotgun with him. I felt like I could finally breathe. I didn't have to be afraid of anyone or anything. The icing on the cake was that his future life plans, of truly creating a village, mirrored the life I had envisioned for myself.

It was no secret to anyone that I dove headfirst into this relationship. After five months of me fantasizing about our forever, I realized just how much he checked off all the hypothetical boxes I held up against him: He loved his family, he had morals, he had a business, and he would lavish me with gifts.

One day, he sent me to the mall with his credit card, which he'd often do whenever he wanted to buy me things. So I bought this beautiful bracelet and a ring.

"I bought a promise ring today," I told him casually after leaving the mall.

"What?!"

"I bought a promise ring. Remember we were talking about it?" I didn't wait for him to answer before I kept explaining what the new ring that shone on my left hand meant. "It means that we're in a relationship and the love that we have and the trust that we're building will lead us to one day be together. With this ring, you're promising to marry me one day."

"All right, Porsha," he said.

I couldn't help but notice a slight annoyance in his voice when he added, "But give me back my credit card. You're doing too much."

Not too long after my trip to the mall, Southern Jon said he wanted to take me to a horse ranch. I had never been to a horse ranch before so I was so excited to go. I was telling my mom and my cousin Tiffany how I had looked it up and we were headed to a romantic bed-and-breakfast, which sounded so quaint because I had never been to one of those before, either.

When we drove up in Jon's truck, it looked even more beautiful than I had imagined. A long winding road led us to a big, beautiful house that was surrounded by six or seven identical smaller cottages all lined up in a row. We stopped at the big house to pick up the keys and meet the owners, a husband and wife who ran the property, before we unloaded our bags and found our own little cottage, filled with charming antique furniture.

Later that night, we had a family-style dinner with the couple, who told us how they acquired the property and managed the horses who were quietly sleeping in a stable beside us.

Jon was being supersweet that night, telling the owners how he was proud of me. And I just remember it being the most amazing dinner I had ever had in my life, down to the mashed potatoes, which were dripping with butter. Maybe it tasted so good because I was so in love and everything felt so perfect. It was so next level I couldn't help my mind from drifting higher, thinking that maybe he was planning to propose.

My suspicions were heightened the next day when the couple took us out on their horses. It was the perfect Georgia day with hardly any humidity as the sun shone brightly down on us. We rode horseback on a picturesque trail into the woods. Riding slowly, we approached an area to stop and have lunch before riding back to our cottage. Under a flower-filled gazebo, we drank chilled champagne and had a bite to eat while looking out at rows and rows of beautiful Georgia trees. It was the perfect day to take in a perfect view with my perfect country boy.

This was back in the day when we didn't take a picture of every single amazing thing that ever happened to us, which forced me to really take it all in. It meant so much to me, and I couldn't have written a more beautiful day.

But I'd have to hold on to the memories of that day because once night fell, so did my relationship. The sun setting gave rise to something deeply hidden within Jon—something that to this day I don't understand.

(For all the women who've had something stolen from them, this is a trigger warning.)

Instead of having dinner at the big house that night, we decided to drive to a local restaurant close by. It was then that I felt a switch had flipped in Jon. Our dinner was nice, but I could tell something was eating away at him. Something was on his mind. Something was bothering him. Just like that, something about my Jon had changed.

I had to pull to hold a conversation with him, which was really odd after all the love and attention he had showered on me earlier that day in the woods. At a dinner where he refused to give me much conversation, we rushed through the meal to head back to our little love cottage—or so I thought. We both stepped into his truck and into a different dimension.

"Oh no, baby, you make a left turn here," I said once I realized he was going the wrong way.

"No," he replied sharply, harshly, keeping his eyes intensely on the road. "We take a right. Stupid!"

At the sound of that word, my entire body lit up and shut down at the same exact time. It felt like someone had just lit my body on fire and I knew, I knew, I knew, nobody would come to put it out.

"Look, I'm sorry," I said, taking the fault immediately. "But what is wrong with you? Why you acting like this? Please!"

I wasn't sure what had made Jon call me that, but back then whenever a guy got upset, I immediately folded. In my twenties, I never wanted to make a man upset. I immediately apologized. I immediately wanted to avoid an argument. I didn't push my point, at all. My only focus was diffusing the situation.

So in that moment, instead of saying, *Okay this is ridiculous, Jon, what the hell are you talking about?* I immediately apologized and backed down.

For some reason, I felt like it was my fault that I'd continued to find myself in these situations. *Why do I let myself be spoken to like this?* I'd ask myself over and over again. *Why do I let myself be taken advantage of?* And if I really allowed myself to answer, I'd say to myself that I was simply happy to be in their presence. I was happy to get their love. I was happy to get their attention. I was happy to just be there.

The worst part about it all is that I never became familiar with accountability. It was a word and an action that I never knew existed. It didn't exist in my relationships. Instead, when the men in my life acted out, I didn't do much about it afterward, but my soul and my spirit were getting worn out.

With the gas light lit up on his dashboard, Jon pulled into a gas station. But it didn't matter what was going on around us, Jon was still in a rage. And here I was, in the eye of the storm with him, trying to avoid stepping in it at all costs.

"I'm sick of this shit. You spent all this money on this ring and I didn't even ask you to. You just took my credit card and bought a ring," he spat out, never looking in my direction.

I had to correct him: "Jon, I didn't take your credit card. You gave it to me. And if it's that big of a deal, I'll take the ring back. It's not that serious. I don't want you arguing with me over a ring. I thought you loved me. I thought you wanted to give me a promise ring."

"Yeah, but I mean you can't just take somebody's credit card and buy a promise ring. We talked about it and the next thing you did was go to the mall and buy one. I didn't even ask you to."

It was true: I showed up at the mall with his credit card, a diamond in my eye, and a dream in my heart. I'm not sure what made me actually calculate how much three months' salary would be for Jon to figure out the size of the diamond he'd eventually buy me. But I wanted so badly to be with him; to get my happily ever after. And more important, to make it happen for myself.

What I didn't realize at the time was that my dream coming to fruition, in the form of a ring, would unintentionally build resentment in Jon's heart. With him wanting to spoil me, he probably thought he couldn't dare say that it was too expensive. Jon turned everything amazing that we had done together and that he had done for me into a scenario, in his mind, where I manipulated or forced him to do it. I somehow had morphed into the mastermind who was taking his money and making plans for his life.

"You stupid bitch…" he said, breaking my train of thought and breaking my entire heart.

Right there in the passenger seat of his car, a place where I'd once felt so loved and so safe and so protected, I now felt completely torn down, ripped apart, cut open. An evilness had opened up inside him and turned the Jon I knew, the Jon I fell in love with, the one who loved family and togetherness and fellowship, into someone who was now raising his voice, being aggressive, and cursing me out. His words smacked the taste of my mouth.

Jon got back into the truck to drive back to our cottage. I thought the piercing silence that now hung in the air would calm him down, but as we were getting closer, I realized that the opposite was happening.

Speeding down the winding dirt roads, Jon was talking to himself under his breath and hitting the steering wheel. I didn't dare say a word to him; I didn't want to escalate or agitate whatever was going on inside his mind.

In the dead of night and in the middle of his wrath, that big, beautiful house at the end of that long winding road now looked like a haunted house. This beautiful plot of land surrounded by quaint antique cottages had now turned into my worst nightmare. There were absolutely no lights on through the property. It was pitch black and the only light that pierced through was from the beams on Jon's truck.

When we finally drove up to our cottage, he turned completely silent. With his headlights now turned off, and the veil now lifted, I turned to Jon, who refused to look at me, and all I saw was a completely dark person. In one car ride, he had become my worst nightmare.

We got out of the truck but he was still not speaking to me—not saying a word—and I was not saying much to him, either. By the time we walked into the cottage and got into the bedroom, I thought he was calming down, but it didn't help how I felt.

Looking around our cottage, which now felt small and claustrophobic, I realized how alone I was. I was out in the middle of nowhere, and I was alone. I was afraid.

I took off my clothes to get ready for bed. As I was taking off my makeup, tying up my hair, and putting on my nightgown, he was still not speaking to me. We lay down in the bed.

"You know what, Jon? I want to go home tomorrow. I really don't appreciate how you treated me tonight. I want to go home tomorrow," I said matter-of-factly.

"You wanna go home? You want to fucking go home?" He seethed with an intense anger I was deathly afraid of.

"Well, yeah. I want to go home," I replied, plainly.

"Okay. Fine."

I grabbed my pillow and inched closer to the edge of the bed. I wanted to sleep as far away from him as possible, but the edge of our cold bed didn't feel far enough. Although I was lying down, I couldn't fall asleep. I was too scared to fall into myself and leave this world, even if it was for my dreams. Those couldn't be sweet enough to lure me into an intoxicating escape. My body was on high alert. And it kept me awake.

I knew it kept Jon awake, too, because ordinarily, he'd be snoring loudly in the middle of the night, but not that night. I knew he was awake. He was just lying there. It was scary.

I forced my body, still unsettled and afraid, to get up and lie down on the little love seat in the living room. I picked up a blanket and put it over myself, hoping it would protect me. Trying to will myself as far away from him as possible, I turned my body into the love seat with my back facing him.

About five minutes later, in the dead of night, Jon said: "So you're just going to sleep over there?"

"Yes, I'm going to sleep over here. Good night."

Time refused to move. The moment refused to budge. And the room was still pitch black. Quiet.

I heard his body get up from the bed and walk over to me, in my self-created refuge. Standing over me, he boomed, "Get back in the bed."

"No, I'm good. I'm staying over here."

"GET BACK IN THE BED!"

"No, I'm sleeping over here. This is too much. I am not sleeping with you tonight," I said, pleading with him, begging him to let whatever was bothering him go.

"GET IN THE BED!"

"Stop it! You're scaring me!"

"Oh, you're scared of me? You're scared of me?"

"Yeah, we're out here alone. You're screaming at me. You're scaring me."

Jon took the blanket that I had draped over me and threw it over my head. *What the hell is he doing? Is he going to suffocate me?* I felt his hands around my thighs, forcing my nightgown up. *Okay. He's going to rape me*, I told myself, bracing myself for what was to come.

Jon was moving really fast.

"No, no, no, no, no, stop. Stop. STOP!"

I pulled the blanket off my head a little bit and I saw Jon's face. It wasn't him. It wasn't the man I had fallen in love with. His face had completely changed. His eyes were typically dark brown, but at this moment they were black. There was no soul in his eyes; nothing. I could not see anything. I didn't see the man that I loved. I knew what was going to happen next.

I felt a rush take over my body. My blanket couldn't stop him. My hands couldn't stop him. My screams couldn't stop him. I screamed and screamed and screamed and then I just stopped. I gave up. I lay there. I went to a place that felt familiar, unfortunately. That place held my fears. That place held my hurt. That place held my pain. That place was pitch black.

How did I get here again? What did I do to deserve this? Why am I so helpless?

He stopped.

I got up, walked back to the bed that we shared, and tried to sleep on its edge; anything to feel far away from him. My body was burning and on fire, but I steadied my breath and tried to remain calm. I dared not react. I dared not show any emotion. I didn't want to wake his evil again.

The next morning, Jon really didn't talk much, and I knew I had to get out of there. I lied and told him I had to go to work. We packed up without saying much to each other to prepare for the drive back to Atlanta. He was acting like it hadn't happened. He was acting like nothing had happened and I was acting that way, too.

Then he showed his hand: "So are you going to break up with me now?"

"No," I lied. "I just need to go to work."

"Well, how do you feel? Are you sure you're not going to break up with me?"

"I'm not," I lied again, fearing that if I said what I was really feeling, he'd bang my face into the window, or worse. "I'm not going to break up with you. I just need to go to work. This weekend, this drama, it was a lot."

As we sped toward Atlanta, my only goal was to get out of his truck alive. I would say whatever I needed to say to calm Jon down. I just needed to get home. There was no Uber back then. I couldn't call anybody. I just wanted to get home. I just wanted to get back to my apartment. Soon, but not soon enough, we pulled up.

Jon asked me again, "Are you sure you're not going to break up with me?"

"No. I'll call you when I leave work," I lied, rushing to open the door and into my apartment.

As soon as I saw his Hummer pull off, I texted him: "Listen, we're done."

It didn't take long for his truck to pull up at my doorstep again. He was screaming, yelling, and kicking my door. He demanded his gifts back. He demanded the promise ring. I didn't know who to call. I was too scared to call the police so I called my friend Kim.

"Porsha, girl, just give him back his stuff."

"No, I don't want to," I told Kim, trying to hold defiantly to whatever dignity I had left in this relationship.

"Porsha."

"No!"

Boom. Boom. Boom. Boom. It was Jon, banging down my door like the damn police. The apartment shook lightly underneath my feet—or maybe that was my body vibrating with fear and anger.

"Okay fine, Kim, I'll leave his stuff on my doorstep. I never want to see his face again."

And that's what I did. I put all his gifts in a bag and texted him to come pick it up from outside my door.

We never spoke again but I wasn't comfortable living in my apartment anymore, even though I loved that apartment. When I received my inheritance money after my grandfather's death, in addition to starting my first daycare, I knew exactly what I wanted to do with that generational blessing. I wanted to move out of my momma's house. I really wanted to show my mom that I could do it all by myself; that I could be independent just as she taught me to be.

I also wanted to show her that I was being responsible with my inheritance, which definitely meant financially, but it felt like so much more than that. With my grandfather finally being laid to rest, it really did feel like it was up to me, and the rest of the family, to keep his legacy alive, and I had a lot to live up to.

I just didn't realize how hard that would be, especially when I was surrounded by men who only saw me as a means to an end—men who wanted to use me. Sometimes it was financially. Other times it was sexually. I wouldn't learn until later just how much my hurt cloaked my entire being, attracting broken men like flies to a cold piece of watermelon, left out on a hot summer's day.

I didn't realize it at the time. I couldn't even see the signs. I couldn't tell that they could sniff my low self-esteem from a mile away. But there they were, men who saw my naïveté, my good credit, and my propensity to never want to fight for too long, feeding their egos and their fucked-up desires for my life. Excuse my profanity, but we gotta call a thing a thing, as Iyanla Vanzant says.

Right before the housing bubble burst, banks were giving out loans to anybody with good credit and a pulse. Thanks to one of those men who targeted me, I took advantage of that. This guy, whom I met right before I started dating Clinton, had convinced me that he wanted to date me and wanted to help me launch my first business. But let's be real: I didn't need his help. I was the one who had the money.

Still, I ended up trusting him, so when he told me one afternoon, "Your credit is good. Let's start investing in properties," I didn't think anything of it.

"Wow, really?" I said, thrilled that this man saw more for me than I saw for myself.

I always knew that I was going to be an entrepreneur, but I figured it'd be in the family business of service—whether it was serving the community or serving underserved families. I didn't think I could be a real estate investor.

I ended up being approved for a $2 million loan, which was surprising to say the very least. But in a strange way, I felt proud that I had gotten approved for so much, not realizing how much they were inflating the loans. I felt investing was a business I could get into to make my mom proud, which is all I ever wanted to do.

I had grown up in my mom's daycare center. I had worked in it since I was seventeen years old, but it was nice to have this other business altogether that I had started on my own, that I could do and show her that I was responsible. Not only was I getting into a new industry, but I was doing it big-dog-style.

Our plan was to purchase two penthouse condominiums, both listed at half a million dollars, in Buckhead, which is an upscale area of Atlanta that reminds you of Fifth Avenue in New York or Beverly

Hills in Los Angeles. I thought, *This is going to show my mom that I am doing it. I'm responsible. I've used my grandfather's money properly and I'm setting up future generations so that I can pass down something to them, too.*

When I went to sign the paperwork to purchase the two condos, I heard a familiar voice right when I was about to sign the last document. By the grace of God I paid attention to this voice, this energy, this ancestor, my gut, my God, telling me *Do not buy two condos.* Something in my spirit told me, *Porsha do not sign that paperwork. Don't. Do not do it. Let that apartment go. Just buy one apartment. Please, Porsha, just buy one.*

So I did just that: I bought a penthouse in Buckhead and rationalized to myself that if I couldn't find renters to pay my mortgage, I could always live in it.

Later, I felt conned by this man who pretended to be interested in me so I would open up my wallet to him. I'd look back on that moment as the one that saved my financial life from legitimate ruin.

This guy ended up being a middleman and paid himself the closing costs on my penthouse condo. He had big talk that we'd run this real estate investing company together, but in reality I would've been stuck with two mortgages and he'd be nowhere to be found.

I wish I could say this was the only time I had been taken advantage of by men—financially, physically, emotionally—but it wasn't. Throughout my twenties, I was forced to continue to protect myself by listening to the guiding voice of God.

* * *

When I touched down in Chicago, I spotted a man holding a sign with my name on it. He was my driver, a light-skinned older man who drove me through the frozen streets of Chicago.

Although the sun was already starting to set, the headlights from his car lit up the streets as we drove farther and farther away from the city's center. They also revealed little snow flurries and eventually a gate that opened as soon as we pulled in on what looked like a mansion.

"There are a lot of girls that come here," my driver said as we neared the house.

I didn't know if he was trying to make conversation or warn me of something, but I'd soon find out.

I thought I was going to a recording studio, but instead we pulled to the side of this huge house. When the car finally stopped in the circular driveway, I opened the door and the driver helped me grab my black Calvin Klein luggage from the trunk. As I walked into the side of the home, a big guy escorted me from the car into what looked like the basement of the home. It almost looked like a security checkpoint because it was a bland all-white room where two guys sat at a table staring at security cameras.

"Hey Porsha! Come on," a familiar voice said.

It was Lenny, the dude who had invited me out here to meet R. Kelly.

I'd randomly met Lenny in the middle of a lounge inside the Bellagio in Las Vegas. I was with some friends, chilling, drinking, minding our business when he slithered over to us, trying to make introductions.

"What do you do? You look like you're on TV," he said, clearly trying to gas me up.

"Noooo, I'm not."

"Well, are you an artist?" he pressed.

"I can sing."

At the time, I honestly didn't know if I could sing or not. But my momma said I could sing so I thought I could sing. She was always encouraging me to use my gifts. So when Lenny asked me if I was an artist, posturing like he could help me make it in the industry, I jumped at the opportunity. I was a singer that day.

"Well, I know R. Kelly, you know, and I could introduce you."

"Really?!" I said excitedly.

"Yeah, he's looking for a new artist. He's got a couple projects that are coming out really soon. You know what? Sing for me right now. Let's see what you got."

"Right…now? At this table?"

"Yeah. Let me hear you sing," Lenny said, crossing his arms to show he was serious.

And in that moment I heard my momma's voice: "If someone ever asks you to sing, you just do it. You sing. You gotta stay ready so you don't gotta get ready." So I did it. I mean, this was an opportunity to work with R. Kelly. This could be great for me. This could be my big break. So I put those butterflies in my stomach inside their cage, stood flat-footed, and sang "His Eye Is on the Sparrow."

"Oh, you got a nice voice. All right. All right."

Everything after that happened so fast. Days after flying back home to Atlanta, I got a call from someone in "R. Kelly's camp" to get my information to book a flight out to Chicago to meet the man I'd later come to know as Robert. When I arrived in Chicago, I thought I'd be staying in a hotel and meeting him at a recording studio, but he had other plans in mind. I was so naive that I didn't realize I was going to a studio…in his house.

I was relieved to see Lenny when I arrived. He'd be the only familiar face I saw all day. After leaving my luggage at security, I followed Lenny inside.

Robert's house had a cabin feel to it. Although the walls were an eggshell color, they were trimmed in cherrywood. We walked down a long hallway where two studios sat across from each other.

"You can sit down right here," Lenny instructed casually.

It was my first time walking into a studio, but I was acting as if I had done this a thousand times. When we finally got a moment to ourselves, I had to ask Lenny what was up.

"You didn't tell me we were going to his house studio!"

Not that it wasn't a state-of-the-art recording studio, but still. This was a really big detail to leave out.

"Oh yeah, yeah, yeah. I meant to tell you," he stammered. "He's got a studio here at his house so this is where we'll be recording. You're going to be meeting Robert in a minute. He's just in the studio across the hall working on something else. Are you nervous?"

"No," I lied. "I'm ready."

I was nervous, but like so many different opportunities in my life, if I believed that it could happen, it would happen. If this opportunity was meant to happen, then I'd be ready for it and it would work out for my good. I never asked, *Why me?* I always asked, *Why not me?*

"All right, cool. I'm just gonna have him play a couple of things and you see what you vibe to."

Lenny left me in the studio to gather my thoughts. Little did I know it would be the last time I saw him. Ever.

I sat in the darkened studio alone thinking, *Oh my God. I'm in R. Kelly's house.* At the time, he was a huge star. He had just released "Trapped in the Closet." It was only a few years after he had released "Happy People," "Ignition," "U Saved Me," and every Black person's cookout anthem back in the day, "Step in the Name of Love." And here I was being personally invited to go meet him. I felt special. I felt like this was my big break. If I could just pull this off, I'd be one step away from "making it."

After a while, I realized I had been waiting for so long that I'd begun to think, *Who knows that I'm here?* I really hadn't told anybody that I had left Atlanta and had flown all the way to Chicago. My gut was telling me to check in, so I pulled out my phone so I could text my girl and let her know I was there. Just in case.

A light knock on the door broke my train of thought. A guy that I had never seen before poked his head into the dimly lit studio. "You can come in here," he said drily, opening the door for me and leading me to a much smaller, yet brighter, studio across the hall.

Robert, wearing dark sunglasses and a hat turned backward, sat in the corner of the studio. Along with the guy who had just led me into the studio to meet him, an engineer sat at the board in the control room.

"Hi, I'm Porsha!" I said brightly, walking up to shake his hand.

"Oh yeah, nice to meet you! Nice to meet you! I heard about

you," he said a little too fast. "You came with Lenny, right? Yeah, I've known him for years. He told me about you. You sing. He said you got a nice voice. Well, I'm working on this music right now. Matter fact, sit down right here. Sit down right here. I want you to hear something."

Robert pointed to a chair right beside him. But that other guy was sitting in it and he didn't budge. Instead, the dude looked at Robert from the side, burying whatever slick thought was in his mind.

"Ay, watch out man! Let her sit down right here," Robert said with a little bit more bass in his voice.

The guy stood up slowly and found another place to land while I sat down in the seat that he had warmed up. When he nodded to the engineer, a song started playing through the studio's speakers. It sounded magical, almost like the pitch-perfect notes were bouncing off the walls. When Robert started singing to the track, it made the song come alive right before my eyes.

Wow, I'm really sitting in the presence of magic and true talent, I thought to myself, slowly bobbing my head along to the beat, trying to fix my face as if I was judging the song with a singer's ear. But in reality, it felt like he was mixing an intoxicating potion. The music was infectious. It filled up the entire studio. It rubbed the nervousness off me. It seemed like it had broken the ice between us.

"This is a song I just wrote off the top of my head," he said. "I'm not one of those people who read and write and stuff like that."

"Yeah, we just produced it a couple of minutes ago," his engineer turned around and added.

"Wow! That's a really great song," I said.

And it was.

Within fifteen minutes, Robert started treating me as if he had known me for years. It was actually kind of disarming to have him suddenly act like we were friends and I was his homie who stopped by to kick it in the studio while he was creating. Although it didn't feel forced on his end, I was pushing to catch up to the moment.

I was there to prove I was ready to take my dreams to the next level, but he never asked me to sing for him. After he played his track, he didn't even talk about music again. I wanted to press him, to fight for my opportunity, but I was scared to. What if I did speak up for myself just to be humiliated? Or worse, what if I was kicked out of his house with no place to go and no way to get home to Atlanta?

I tried to rationalize the moment: Even if I didn't do a song with him, at least I was present for this song. Even if we never got around to working on music for me, at least I was here for this…and what a privilege.

As I was in the studio kicking it and chilling, it dawned on me that I hadn't seen Lenny in hours and I had no idea where I was staying. I had two rollaway pieces of luggage that I had left at the security checkpoint and had no clue who to ask about which hotel I was staying at. I was nervous to ask because I didn't want to seem like I was uncomfortable.

I wasn't. We were all watching a small television mounted in the studio while making small talk. Robert even complained about an interview he had just done where the reporter had irritated him over some personal question, and we all laughed about it. He wasn't hitting on me. Not yet, at least. He was relaxed, cool, chill. He treated me like a friend.

After a couple of hours, Robert stood up and said, "I'll be back," and he left. His friend, the one who had led me in the studio hours ago, followed him. I was left in the studio with the engineer, whose back was toward me.

I sat there for about forty-five minutes, keeping my eyes glued to the television, confused. Eventually, another random guy whom I had never seen before came into the studio and said, "Oh, Porsha, you can come with me. I can show you where you can put your stuff."

"Okay. Cool," I said, standing up, relieved that I didn't have to sit in that studio anymore.

As I looked around at the cabin-like mansion, wide eyed, trying to take everything in, I walked through the home and up a flight of stairs. I was rationalizing to myself: *He must be putting me up for the night in a guest room. Maybe I'm going to stay here and we'll work in the studio tomorrow.*

I was desperately trying to figure out what in the world was going on while not trying to rock the boat. It was a skill I learned early on in my life, wanting to be liked, wanting people to like me, wanting to please, wanting to go along to get along. It rarely served me, but in my mind, it was better than living in conflict.

"You can just stay here in the house or whatever," the guy said, casually. "Robert will see you later."

With a house this size, I figured he probably had two or three guest bedrooms so I didn't mind staying here before my flight the next day. But when this guy opened the double doors, I got the sense that he had just walked me into the master bedroom: Robert's bedroom.

As I tiptoed into his huge bedroom, my thoughts rushed into my brain, bumping into one another. They were trying to make sense of everything I had ever said to Lenny, to Robert, to everyone. Could anyone have gotten the impression that I had come here for anything other than music? No, no! I was naive, sure, but professional nonetheless. I didn't even know how I ended up here or how was I going to get out.

I looked around what was so obviously his bedroom, with a poster bed that sat in the middle of the room. Around it sat an entire living room set up complete with a couch. The room was so huge, it also fit a table and set of chairs.

What was I supposed to do in here? I wasn't sure what I would do to pass the time, but as the minutes turned into hours, and after what was on the television could no longer distract me from this surreal experience, I looked out the bay window. I couldn't tell what time of day it was, but my body let me know it was sometime in between the thick of night and the dawn of morning. I peeked my head out the bedroom door and looked down the hall. I noticed a photo of his ex-wife hung in the hallway, and thought to myself, *Is he still married?*

"I'm so sorry, baby," Robert said, walking in the door and talking to me as if we were in a relationship, a stark difference from how he treated me earlier in the studio. "I wanted us to work later, but I got caught up."

When I heard his voice, I reluctantly opened my eyes, realizing I had drifted off to sleep. I looked around the room, trying to process exactly where I was. I still couldn't believe I was actually in R. Kelly's bedroom. How had I let it get this far? I had no idea what was in store, but I played along.

"Oh, that's okay. It's all right," I said.

Robert immediately started kissing me.

"I'm really into you. I think you're beautiful," he said. "I'm just looking for somebody that I can spend time with. I need a girlfriend, a girl who's mature and patient and keeps a low profile. I need her. Can you be that girl?"

"I'm super low key," I replied. I felt myself getting caught up in the fantasy, as if I was dreaming. "But what about your wife?"

"I'm single," he emphasized. "And I'm lonely all the time."

Robert said he spent so much time by himself because he worked so much on his craft, and when he was working it was not only hard for him to meet people, but also hard to be around people. He acted like his gift was just so heavy on him that whenever it called for him to be in the studio that's what he had to do. That need, that pull, it kept him from a lot of relationships in his life. Robert said he just needed somebody who would be understanding of what he could give in a relationship and what he could not.

Hearing Robert pour his heart out, it made me want to be that for him. It was the way he opened up—needing me, wanting me—that made me want to be there for him. I wanted to be that girl that he was looking for, to live that fairy tale.

But my rational mind kept pulling on me, too. It begged me to question what was going on, and it'd continue to pull me back and forth throughout the next few months.

"So y'all not together?" I pressed.

"No, we're not together."

"Oh, okay, because I saw her picture. In the hallway."

"We're not together. We haven't been together for a long time. It's just me. It's just me and my kids. I just like your spirit. It's something about you," he said, promptly changing the subject. "I want you to take your clothes off."

My rational mind woke back up at that line. I could've laughed in his face, grabbed my luggage, and walked right out of there. I liked to think I would have if I wasn't in the middle of nowhere with nowhere to go. Or I could do what I had done in so many situations and put what I felt—nervousness mixed with panic—to the side in order to survive what was about to happen.

Plus I'm already here, I told myself. I'm in his bedroom. *I've already been in his house for hours. It's three or four in the morning. I've already put myself in this position. This is what you're supposed to do. You have to. You have to. There is no turning back. What are you gonna do, say no and then what? Then you're stranded with nowhere to go.*

So I took off my clothes while he stood there looking at me. At that time, my body wasn't the body I have now. I was skinny, no more than 145 pounds. My body looked very young. I had no breasts, no hips, but he didn't seem to mind. In fact, it seemed to turn him on.

"How old are you?" he asked.

"Twenty—" I replied before he cut me off from finishing saying my age, which was twenty-five.

"Stop," he said. "Let's just say you're very young."

A few minutes later I ran to the bathroom to wash him off me. I felt so disconnected from the man who had just told me how badly he needed me. I turned the sink on so he couldn't hear what I was doing. When I walked back out, his shirt was back on.

"You're good?" Robert said, looking over at me. "I gotta go. I'm supposed to be meeting this producer."

It was around five or six in the morning, but I just let him tell me any excuse to leave. And he left.

What I didn't realize when he walked through his double doors was that he'd leave me in his bedroom for the entire next day. The door wasn't locked, yet I didn't feel welcome to roam around his house alone. He never told me I couldn't leave, but he also never encouraged me to make myself at home. He never told me not to open the door, but he also never invited me downstairs to get something to eat. By simply leaving me there, he'd disarmed me. I was frozen.

I eventually got up the courage to call downstairs because I was starving. I needed something to eat. Thoughts of working on music sat in my mind, and that's where they'd lie dormant.

By the time Robert walked back into his bedroom, with me still lying on the bed watching television so many hours later, I was just happy to see someone. I was actually happy to see him.

"I can't believe you left me like that," I told him. "You did it a second time. I don't like to be left alone. I want to go home."

"No, no, no baby, don't be like that," he said, looking genuinely hurt by the mention of leaving. "Let me give you some money. You can go to the mall. Get out of the house."

I had a business and my own money. I had friends, a loving family, and a mother who had taught me better than this back home who would worry about my whereabouts. I thought about my mom a lot when I was at Robert's house and the idea of disappointing her and letting her down kept pulling me back to my senses and calling me home.

I flew back to Atlanta that evening. I never said goodbye to Robert during my first trip to his house, but I'd end up back there two or so more times. I was lured because I was young and insecure. I was lured because of his kind words and loving actions. I was lured because the combination of these two things manipulated me to my core. Each time I went, it got worse and worse and worse.

Robert invited me to fly back out to Chicago through an email I knew he didn't write. When one of his drivers pulled me into his Olympia Fields estate for the second time, security led me straight to a small guest room.

I walked into the yellowish-painted room, which was nestled beside the billiard room where the pool table sat, and again Robert was nowhere to be found. Instead, I was left to stay in that room until he visited me. And again, the door wasn't locked. No one told me I couldn't leave, but it still felt like I wasn't allowed to walk around the house. I felt like I was on lockdown.

I wish I could say this was a new feeling, being trapped in a room, but it wasn't.

The walls eventually started to close in on me after a day and I sneaked out of the room to get some fresh air. On my way back from the pool area, where I passed a security guard who invited me to swim if I wanted to, I bumped into a really pretty light-skinned girl in the hallway. She wasn't wearing any makeup, and her hair was slicked back into a ponytail. She made eye contact with me.

"Hey," she whispered.

Matching her tone, I replied back whispering, "Hey! I'm Porsha. I'm over here in this room."

"I'm down the hall."

"How many girls are here?"

"I don't even know."

Suddenly, one of the big security guards made his way into the hallway. "Oh yeah, you can go into your room right there, right there," he said, motioning to her.

Immediately, without another word, and without making any eye contact with me, she disappeared.

"You shouldn't talk to her," he warned me.

Robert eventually came to visit me in my room a day later, with apologies dripping from his lips. "I'm sorry. I was working. You know how it be. Listen, come out with me. Come out the room. Let's go get something to eat. My family is having a cookout."

He led me downstairs to the family room where his entire family was relaxing—running back and forth from the kitchen, eating, and chilling. Robert's aunt, whom I had never met but who somehow knew my name, was there, too.

"Hey, Porsha!" she said as if she knew me. "Go ahead and fix yourself a plate."

By this time it was my second day in the room with nothing to eat. I was so hungry. So I ran into the kitchen and piled food on my plate, but when I got to the potato salad, I paused. It was the most yellow potato salad I had ever seen. *Wow, is this how they make their potato salad in Chicago with all this mustard?* I thought. I was hungry, but I wasn't that hungry. You can't eat everybody's potato salad anyway.

Before I sat back down with the rest of his family, I heard a voice say, "Oh, you're such a pretty girl. Robert did good with you. Robert! Robert! Yeah, man you did good with her."

It was his sister.

"Oh yeah, I love her," he replied to her. Eventually, he turned his head to me and said, "Porsha, I love you, man. You know I'm gon' have a baby by you, right? Did y'all know that?"

His family either ignored us or looked at us in admiration.

Robert laid his head in my lap and I immediately forgot about all the anger I felt after being locked up in the room all day. Being around Robert, being wrapped up in his fantasies, made you want to believe in his fantasies, too. Even if you knew better.

This moment overrode any logic I understood about what was happening inside that house. I wanted to believe I wasn't a girl he was locking in his room to use whenever he wanted or remembered. This was public confirmation, in front of his whole family, that he loved me, or at least he thought he did. I chose the fantasy of security and love and family over what was actually happening to me. Because the one thing I always wanted was to be loved, and that's what he was giving me.

Even with my own business, a supportive family and friends, I only saw myself through his eyes…and I didn't see much.

I didn't stay for long during that second trip, but Robert would call often. When he did call, I felt like we were in some kind of relationship, even if our interactions and conversations were sporadic and a bit random.

I was settled back in Atlanta when I received a phone call from Robert inviting me back out to Chicago. He came with more and more apologies, his signature refrain, telling me, "I'm so sorry I left you in the room like that. I'll never do that again. I love you. We're supposed to be starting a family." Although my gut was telling me to leave this man alone, I unfortunately ignored it one last time.

I had touched down in Chicago and once again slipped into the backseat of a private car, and once again I was greeted by security at the side door. This time, I was led to a completely different room in a different part of the estate.

I found myself in a fully mirrored room. Aside from the hardwood floors, the room was entirely covered in reflective mirrors. It had mirrors on every wall and mirrors on the ceiling. The only part of the wall that wasn't reflective was where the television was mounted. I thought to myself, *This is going to be rough*.

I was left in that room, staring at different versions of myself, for three days straight. Or it might've been two days straight. When you're left alone in a room like that for long, you lose track of time. Thankfully, I had brought my laptop with me. If I was going to be on lockdown, I needed something to distract me. I also made sure to tell a girlfriend I was at his house, just in case.

I'll never understand how I let him lure me back to his house time and time again only to be locked away. I'll never understand why I was afraid to leave. And each time I wanted to be like, *You know what? I'm getting out of here*, Robert or a security guard would pop up, luring me back and convincing me to stay.

After twenty-four hours of staring at myself in those mirrors, I called downstairs to the security desk to say I wanted to leave. I was done.

"Well, Porsha, Robert says he wants you to be ready in an hour. He wants you to go to a party with him."

"He does?"

"Yes, he does. Can you be ready in an hour? Wear minimal makeup."

If I could turn back the clock, I wish I had the strength I have now to say no. But instead, I got dressed and followed a security guard down to a large room inside his estate that held a pool table in the middle of the floor. When I walked inside the room, there were about twenty or thirty other girls in there—all different types. A speaker that I couldn't see played one of his songs. Robert's songs were the only ones we'd hear all night.

What kind of party is this? Where did these girls even come from? I wondered.

I walked up to a few girls to make conversation, to have something to do, to pass the time. I mean, I hadn't seen or spoken to anyone since I'd arrived. I also wanted to figure out if these girls were staying in his house, too, or if I was the only one.

"I've been here a month," one said.

"I've been here a week," another whispered.

"I'm staying in the studio," yet another girl shared. "I'm actually still in school."

About an hour into the "party," Robert strolled in like he was the star of the night. All the girls started clapping and yelling and saying stuff like, "Ooooh! R. Kelly! There he is! Oooh."

"Hey ladies! Thank you for being here tonight," Robert said after walking to the center of the room, near the pool table. "I just wanted us to all have a way to get together and have a good time."

With that he started to mingle with each girl. While some girls, in baggy clothes, didn't speak to anyone, others were trying desperately to get into the party spirit. Everyone, though, was vying to get a little attention from Robert.

Eventually, he came over to say hello to me. "Hey, Porsha baby," he said, giving me a kiss on the lips. I didn't see him kiss anybody else on the lips so perhaps I was his girlfriend after all—his girlfriend in a pretty messed-up relationship.

The "party" ended after Robert left the room with two cute girls who had kept to themselves for most of the night. Of course I was upset about it, but what did I expect after being in a room full of girls throwing themselves at him?

I dragged myself back to that spooky mirrored room, feeling worthless. I was beyond upset; I was sad. I was depressed and the worst part about it was that I wasn't even that upset with him. I felt more disappointed in myself that I had found myself in this place, at this party, with these girls. When I wasn't distracted by him, I was being tortured by questions that clouded my mind.

What is my life? Why am I okay with this? Why am I okay with him treating me like this? How did I get into this situation? What would have led me to this place? If I'm so afraid of being here, why do I continue to stay here? What is keeping me here?

It was as if I had suddenly snapped awake. I had to get out of there. I picked up the phone in the room, dialed zero, and was patched in to the security desk.

"I gotta go."

"But he's gonna come soon," they said, trying to dissuade me. "He's coming. He's coming."

"Is he gonna come soon?" I pressed.

"He's coming."

But he never did. Hours and hours and more hours rolled by. With every second and every minute, the nerve that I had just mustered up became even more lackluster. I was back in this hole again with nowhere to go and no one to tell me this was not okay.

My boredom lured me into a nap, but it didn't last long. I was woken by a guttural scream; a sound of true terror. From the inside of my mirrored hell, the sounds were muffled but they were distinct enough that I could tell a girl was crying out. A man was screaming, too, and it sounded like Robert, but I couldn't be sure.

I heard a man's voice say loud and clear, "What the fuck? You got me fucked up." I soon heard loud footsteps shuffling around as if they were running followed by a loud thump. Something, or someone, had fallen. Then it sounded like a woman was getting beaten and every time a fist landed, she'd let out a pathetic yet energetic cry. It was terrifying.

I picked up the phone immediately and dialed security. My nerve had returned. I didn't dare let them talk me out of leaving this time.

"If you don't change my flight right now and get me out of here, I'm calling the police. Now."

I slammed down the receiver and called the one girlfriend who knew I was here. Still fearful about what was happening in that house, I whispered into the phone to tell her what was going on.

"Don't worry, Porsha. We're getting you out of there. I can check on flights, too."

Thank God she did, pointing out a few flights that would get me back to Atlanta by nightfall. But by the time I had gotten off the phone with her, security was already calling me back telling me, "Your car is downstairs. You can go to the airport."

Over the next two weeks, Robert called a few times. Most times I let the calls go to voicemail, until I couldn't take it anymore.

"Please don't call me anymore. I'm done with you."

Fast forward to years later, I sat down with investigators to tell them my story. I never in a million years thought there would be an opportunity for me to tell my truth to officials. I had kept this experience so very close to the chest to protect myself. Even my own mother didn't know the depths of what had happened in R. Kelly's house; I had just worked up the nerve to tell her about some of it only a few years ago.

I spoke up. I felt like I had to, especially when I heard about R. Kelly's victims. I was touched by their heartbreaking stories and if I could do anything to help them or their families, I wanted to. If I could help someone who was still trying to come forward by sitting down with them, I wanted to be able to do that, too. Together, our team helped with the investigation, which I was more than happy to do.

I couldn't believe what had just happened. I thought, *Wow, I've never said any of that aloud.* The past had just walked back into my life, bringing all those moments right back to my mind and those emotions right back to my heart.

It took me right back to being in that mirrored room and wondering what was going on with me that I'd allowed myself to be in that situation. At forty, I wish I could turn back the clock and talk to my younger self and see the value of who I was. I share this story now for every person reading this book, so that you can find your power and purpose to walk away.

CHAPTER FIVE

My feet hurt.

It was another Friday night and I was in the club. It wasn't my first time at Tongue & Groove in Buckhead, so I managed to skip the line and walk right in, my stilettos barely hitting the pavement as the valet parked my car.

The air inside Tongue & Groove was a mix of weed, sweat, and the strongest colognes and perfumes all mixed together in a late-night concoction, but somehow it still smelled sweet. My girl and I were weaving around men, who were steadily grasping at our waists and lightly brushing our butts as if we didn't feel it, making our way to the bar.

We ordered our first round of drinks and tried to sip them slow, to make them last a little bit longer. All the while I was acting like I wasn't sucking in my stomach in this skintight bodycon dress.

My friend was acting like a little butterfly that evening and could never settle on a place to land inside the club. I opted to hug the bar a bit tighter, not wanting to take up more space in the room, even though I wasn't really a big drinker back then.

What am I doing here? No seriously, why am I here?

The deejay played the same songs he'd played last month, in the same rotation. And the crowd seemed to jump in *Ayyyy*s and *That's my song* at the same parts.

Hoping to get back to my friend, I left the comfort of the bar and looked for her around the club. As I walked across the middle of the dance floor, I felt my body stop all of a sudden. My eyes were wide open, but everything went pitch black. And I knew it wasn't the alcohol because I had only had a couple of drinks. This was different. It was supernatural.

Drowning out the bass-heavy songs that vibrated through the tucked-away speakers surrounding me, a voice said to me very clearly: *Come out from where you are so you can bring them to me.*

I wasn't shocked or even scared to hear God's voice. It was the most familiar voice I had ever heard, almost like my own. And honestly, I was relieved, because after years of speaking to God, pleading with Him, and asking Him so many questions I had for my life, He had finally answered.

Like many sacred things in my life, I found God thanks to my mother. Although I had known God all my life, since like every other Black person in Atlanta I had grown up in the church, it wasn't until my late twenties that I truly took the time to get to know Him and allowed Him the opportunity to get to know me, even though He already knew every intricate part of my being. And more than that, He had designed me to serve Him, to honor Him, to worship Him.

In my twenties, my mother became serious about attending a Baptist church in Atlanta and began serving God through evangelism. So I started becoming serious, too, especially after finding myself in so many uncomfortable situations. I needed a divine reset.

We went to church every single Sunday and many days in between. I would spend weekends at convocation. I went to every revival. If my pastor was a guest preacher at another church in the area, I'd follow him to that church to support him. I even joined the praise team, trying to worship with every gift I possessed.

I'll never forget singing with the praise team because although I could carry a tune and harmonize, I would be so nervous. It didn't help that one Sunday the choir director wanted all of us to sing a solo.

Now, I didn't mind singing a solo in front of our small church of about fifty people, but that Sunday the church was packed! There were even people standing up in the back because there was nowhere to sit down, thanks to the guest prophet preaching that day, who had brought his entire congregation with him. *Great! Now I'm going to have to sing in front of all of these people. I am not ready*, I thought to myself.

I was standing up there, right at the foot of the pulpit, and I was the last one to do my solo. But every time another member of the praise team sang, it just made me even more and more nervous to do my part. I wasn't paying attention. I wasn't in the spirit. I was just trying to talk myself up so I wouldn't have a panic attack when I sang the first note.

When the song finally got to my part, I could barely breathe, let alone sing. I might've let out a Jeeeeeesus but by the time I finished singing His name, I was on the floor. I kid you not. I saw blackness and I literally hit the floor. I passed completely out. Not a little bit; no. Out!

When I came to, all I heard around me was my church family saying, "The Holy Ghost done got Porsha. Praise Him! Praise Him!" They were fanning me and making sure I was okay. Meanwhile, to cover up my embarrassment, I hopped up and joined the rest of the congregation, saying, "Jesus saved me! Jesus saved me!"

God, please forgive me.

Still, for years, I went to work and went to church, went to work and went to church. That was it and it was everything to me. I found so much joy in His word and His promises. I found a safeness I desperately needed and a comfort I craved.

I had grown so much in my relationship with God that it had transformed into an actual relationship. It was more fulfilling than any job, any man, any drink, any drug, any shopping spree. He was more than enough. He was greater. He was my comfort. He was my peace.

If at any time I felt stress, I didn't worry about it. Because I believed, just as God's word said, that He had my back. God was my mother. God was my father, and I knew that He'd turn any situation around for my good. I believed all of it, every word, every scripture. I literally felt, and still feel, like I am God's child.

With God, I didn't have to feel ashamed of anything in my past like when dreams were violently stripped from me, or when my humanity was literally wrestled away from me. With God, I could forgive myself for the choices I had made; the men I chose who only disappointed me. With God, I could set myself free. I could break the chains of regret, shame, and guilt to reimagine a life filled with purpose, contentment, and clarity.

So I had been talking to God a lot during that time of my life, asking Him a lot of questions about my life and what He wanted from me. I wanted to know what God needed me to do. How could I please Him? How could I be right so that when I walked through Heaven's doors He (or She, for that matter) could look me in the eye and say, *Porsha, well done?*

But it didn't mean that I let church, or that confining religious lifestyle with its hypocritical judgments and shaming techniques, change who I was or how I carried myself. Well, in many ways it did, the best ways, but what I mean is that I truly believed that God loved me just as I was.

I still wore makeup. I still wore clothes that fit my body despite getting in "trouble" for wearing skirts that were too tight for church because I knew my heart wasn't being disrespectful. God literally made me curvaceous. The women in my church would have their skirts down to their ankles, but I just never felt like I needed to change who I was to be what God needed me to be. I always felt like God had chosen me for who I am and He wanted to use me just the way I am. With some tweaks, I knew that I would be most useful to Him by simply being me.

Spiritually, the biggest struggle that I had was with my own flesh. It's probably the thing I've been battling my whole life. I would always ask God to cleanse me of my flesh, give me a clean heart, and make my spirit stronger. When you ask God for that, because He's faithful, it's going to happen. God was now making my spirit stronger than my flesh; a flesh that had, at times, encouraged me to make poor decisions, persuaded me to say yes when I really wanted to say no, and introduced me to demons that didn't deserve my presence.

Thank God for His unchanging favor.

So in that moment, when God spoke to me on the dance floor in the middle of the club, it didn't scare me. If anything, it was confirmation. I was so thankful that after years of praying to Him, thinking of Him, and speaking to Him, He was finally speaking back for the first time. I was finally at a place in my life where I wasn't distracted, and that's saying a lot since I was literally standing in a crowded nightclub with strobe lights blinking and songs thumping.

I had been here, in the club, countless nights before, watching the evening slip away, letting the hours roll by so I could forget about that ex, that hurt, that parent at the daycare center, my dad. I kept running to the club hoping it would help me forget about all the things that storm my brain at night, haunting me, trying to find answers that I simply didn't have or maybe didn't want to have. Questions that I dared not ask because I was afraid of the answer.

But after years of running away from the questions, they still seemed to find me. It was almost like I had left the front door open and those questions would just walk right in and sit down, staring me in the face. They'd cuddle up with me after a long day at work, pouring their own drink. Dark liquor. The questions prodded me to interrogate my pain and think deeply about my purpose and my destiny. They felt impossible to answer yet relentless in their quest.

Before tonight, inside this club, those questions went from being a suggestive whisper every now and then to a loud nagging request: *Why are you here? What are you looking for? How did you get here? Don't you want something more for your life? Do you think you'll find it without me?*

Perhaps it was my walk with God that gave me the courage to face myself for the very first time, to unmask what I'd rather keep hidden. Even in the neon iridescent lights of the club, I couldn't run away from myself any longer. Believe me, I had tried: I had tried to hide away my pain with nights out, by drinking dark liquor, between someone's legs, and even with shopping. But that pulsating feeling that I was missing out on my purpose, to serve myself and others in a way that pleased Him, had grown too large to ignore. I had to stop running. I had to.

After hearing God's voice, I simply said, *Okay. I hear you.*

I blinked and I was back inside the club, feeling like I had been dropped back inside my life, but feeling distinctly different about everything that I saw around me. The women grinding up against the men, the groomsmen taking shots at the bar, the D-cup bartender who was intentionally leaning over while making drinks. It didn't bother me before God's voice had spoken to me, but now I saw everything with fresh eyes and I couldn't stand any of it.

I instantly felt like I was in a place where I wasn't supposed to be. I immediately saw sin all around me. I had to leave.

The next morning, after chugging water and trying to wipe the night's makeup off with wipes, I turned to the one woman who I knew wouldn't judge me for who I was and where I was.

"Mom, I just had an epiphany," I told her, reaching for more electrolytes to ward off any hangover that had my name on it.

"I was standing in the club last night and I was looking at everyone there. Like, what are we doing? What are we really here for?"

"Well, what do you mean, Porsha?" my momma said, her voice dripping in honeyed understanding while she wiped down the counters in her kitchen.

"I'm not sure what I mean, but last night in that club, listening to the same songs and seeing the same people, I just decided the club life isn't for me anymore. I don't want to be single anymore. I'm ready to be married. Are we supposed to be going out partying or are we supposed to be looking for something more?"

"Yeah, but Porsha, you still have plenty of time to settle down and get married. You're only twenty-six. You don't have to rush it just because you're sick of going out."

"But it's not that. It's not the going-out part that has me questioning everything. I'm sick of not having protection and a special someone to share my life's moments with, to share my successes with. I want a husband. Well no, let me rephrase that: I want to be a wife."

"Well, if you're serious about it, Porsha," my mother began, sensing my sincerity, "you only have to have a heart for it and let God take care of the rest."

Walking into church the next Sunday, I still had what God told me inside the club on my heart. While singing on the four-person praise team inside my small Baptist church in Ellenwood, I couldn't get that moment out of my head. My moment with God was stuck with me even after the pastor told our small church to stand in line and "tell the Lord what you want."

There were fifty or so people sitting on either side of the aisle in wooden pews, but I didn't see them as I walked up to my pastor, whispering in his ear what God laid on my heart. I asked God for a husband.

"Church family!" the pastor boomed into the mic as I stared down at the church's red carpet. "Porsha, here, asked God for a husband. So let's all touch and agree that she finds the man that God has set aside for her. Amen, church? Amen!"

I felt my body melt to the floor from embarrassment. How could the pastor say this aloud?! I was only telling the Lord, not the entire congregation! Lord have mercy!

But I told the Lord what I wanted and a year later there he was.

* * *

It was like he was sent to me. It felt like he was the answer to what I had been yearning for. He was literally what I had been praying for. About a year after I asked God for a husband, I met Kordell Stewart. I know it sounds unbelievable, but it's true. Literally one year after whispering in my pastor's ear, He gave me the desires of my heart.

I didn't even want to be in the club that night. If it wasn't for my friend's birthday, I would've been in the house, watching something that I love on the TV or listening to my favorite music. It was even raining outside, so you know I loved this girl because Black people do not go out in the rain. I definitely wasn't going to the club anymore. I knew there was nothing out there for me.

So there I was reluctantly standing there, talking to a couple of friends I spotted on the dance floor, when I felt someone staring at me from across the room. His eyes were piercing through the crowd. I felt them instantly. *Why is this dude just staring me down? What is going on?*

I met his eye, thinking that my audacity would break his stare, but he just continued looking at me. When I finally looked at him, it felt like I was starring in one of those romantic comedies when you meet somebody's eye and everybody around you disappears and it just feels like you and that person are the only ones left in the room. That's how I felt; it felt like he and I were standing there, staring into each other's eyes on an empty dance floor.

"My friend is interested in you," I heard a man say, breaking my gaze at this handsome man wearing a collared shirt laid wide open. A little too wide; think disco.

"So tell him to come talk to me," I replied, already knowing what was about to happen next.

"He's a little shy," his friend pressed.

"He's shy?! Well, I'm not gonna talk to him through you."

I could tell he wasn't actually shy. I just didn't know why he was reenacting this "shy guy" routine from *The Five Heartbeats*. It was cute.

Eventually, Kordell came over as I predicted he would.

"I'm sorry I didn't come over at first," he said in a deep voice, tinged with a Southern sensibility, "but I think you're very beautiful."

Kordell was from New Orleans. He was a manly man, which meant he was a little intimidating to a lot of people, for sure. I could tell he was an athlete or used to be an athlete. He had the type of body that couldn't hide. He was ten years older than me, so that probably explained the clothes, but I didn't mind it.

He had a strong presence. He had a great voice with a smooth tone. It was perfect for his gig as an ESPN correspondent, which he had scored after leaving the NFL, where he had played for eleven years. He was an athlete so he had a beautiful body…even with his clothes on. He definitely knew how to hang a suit.

He wasn't super-religious, but he was definitely spiritual and he didn't mind that I was religious. We wanted the same things out of life. We both wanted family. We wanted to be more than what they told us we could be. We wanted it all. At times, we felt like we had it.

On our first date, which was at his favorite restaurant, Fleming's in Duluth, Kordell picked me up from my condo. I remember being so charmed by it all because it was so old school and so romantic and so perfect.

I don't remember what we spoke about during that first dinner, but I do remember feeling like Kordell was really listening to me, like really hearing me. I felt like he really saw me. He got me.

So when he told me during that date that he was single and never wanted to get married, I didn't pay any attention to him because what he didn't know was that in that moment, God had already told me he was going to be my husband. I felt so safe, so comfortable, so secure.

Kordell always wanted to be around me and when he wasn't around me he always wanted to know where I was. At the time, I loved that he cared so much about where I was and who I was with. It made me feel protected. Because I craved comfort and covering, I didn't realize it was a red flag.

I'll never forget I was headed out to eat with my cousin Tiffany a few months, maybe six or seven, into our relationship. He had asked me where I was going and I told him, but that didn't stop him from blowing my phone up that night. I mean, he called me back-to-back every five minutes to the point where I had to apologize to Tiffany: "I'm so sorry, girl. I don't know why he's acting like this. I told him I was with you."

I even picked up his phone call once during the evening like, "Hey babe. Everything all right? Remember, I'm with Tiffany."

Here he goes, booming from the other side of the phone: "I know! But y'all are just out too late, Porsha! What are you still doing out, eating at ten o'clock at night?!"

Kordell was yelling so loudly surely my cousin could hear him sitting beside me at the table. I was so embarrassed by his behavior I hung up on him. There was no rationalizing it. There was no reasoning with him.

But I straight up ignored the warning signs because I could rationalize it. *Well, he loves me. He's just looking out for me. He cares for me.* Kordell felt like the first man in a long time who was really invested in me and my future.

I was still having a few bumps with my daycare and trying to make payroll while expanding the business and after venting one evening, I remember him asking me, "What's going on with your business, Porsha? Why is it so disorganized? Why is everything upside down? Why is it difficult for you to pay your workers sometimes? And it's hard for you to make rent? What's happening?"

But he didn't say it in a way to make me feel bad or ashamed. He truly wanted to know and he wanted to help. He came over that night and went through all my mail, and my bills, and wrote out a budget.

He didn't just hand me money to help me out, like other men in my life had done in the past; he patiently mentored me. He felt invested in me from the very beginning. He didn't throw money at me. He was really trying to make me a better businesswoman.

Kordell was giving, too. I mean, this was a man who—when we were eventually engaged—flew me to Vegas and dropped $80,000 on me just because. He wanted me to have the dream; the life.

He also loved being around my family and so if that meant going to church with us, he didn't mind coming and sharing in the word with me, which made him extremely attractive to me.

I knew it was getting serious with Kordell when I brought him over to my mother's house to meet her. Because my mother knows me so well, she could easily tell me if this man was wasting my time or if he was the real deal.

When Kordell walked through the door, he immediately hugged my mother. We were giggly, almost like teenagers, around each other back then. When I looked at him, he looked right back at me, piercing me to my soul—even around my momma.

I remember after church one day, we went over to my mother's house for Sunday dinner. While the food finished simmering, we sat on my mother's yellow sofa. Well, really I sat on the sofa. Kordell ended up sitting at my feet, on the floor, next to me. He looked at me with such admiration in his penetrating eyes.

I felt like Kordell saw me like no other man had seen me before— as a wife, as a mother, and more important as a woman deserving of his attention. And I just cherished him for seeing me for the woman I felt destined to become.

Still, it wasn't long before I started noticing a pattern. Kordell would take me out at a certain time of night. He'd only take me to dark bars or we'd go somewhere where there weren't a lot of people. At first, I didn't really think about it because I was just happy to be with him. I was enjoying his company. I didn't care if we were the only people in the restaurant, sitting in a corner booth with our backs toward the door. But after a while, I started to notice that it felt intentional…almost as if he was hiding me.

We were at The Bucket Shop Cafe in Buckhead, tucked in a corner of the sports bar nestled into one of their huge brown leather booths, when I had had enough.

"It kinda feels like you're hiding me."

"No! I'm not," he said, acting incredulous.

"I know you have a son, though. Are you still with your son's mother or something? What's her name? It's Brandy, right? Seriously. What's up?"

Kordell wasn't shy about speaking about his ex. I knew they had been together for a long time. I knew he had messed up their relationship somehow and felt regretful. I knew too much about them, actually, but I figured he was one of those guys who just talks too much about his last relationship.

You know what? Maybe he's still getting over her. It's fresh, I rationalized. *It's cool. I can be his support system. It's aggravating, but I can be there for him while he works this out. It's okay.*

But it wasn't okay, not really. So I called him after that hide-and-seek date and told him I was breaking it off. I didn't want to date him anymore despite what God had told me. Any man who was hiding me and trying to keep me a secret wasn't the man for me.

But he begged and he pleaded.

"No, no, no come up to my place. You can see there's nothing here. I live alone. I just have one son with my baby's mom."

So I went over there. It wasn't like it was a long trek. Come to find out, Kordell had lived across the street from me in a different condo and oddly enough, I had never seen him or heard of him before we met that fateful night in the club. He had been there just as long as I had been there, but we had been living and running in opposite directions. He went to Publix and I went to Kroger. He went to SunTrust and I went to Bank of America. We thought it was an insane coincidence, but I took it a step further. For me, it felt like destiny.

I went over there and immediately when I walked in his door, I saw the most beautiful flowers on his cocktail table. There were two dozen long-stem red roses standing in a glass vase. I couldn't believe how thoughtful and caring he was, and I couldn't hide my excitement. I ran straight over to the flowers, wanting to smell them one by one.

"Oh my gosh, Kordell! These are beautiful! Oh, wow!"

I picked up the card delicately placed beside the vase and began to read it. The card said, "Thank you for everything. I appreciate you so much."

Wait. What? I didn't get it. Thank you, for what? I was confused for a split second until my instincts took over from where my brain left off. *These flowers aren't for me. Oh my God. These flowers aren't for me. They're for him. They're from a woman. They're from his ex. This asshole left these flowers here by mistake because these are from his baby's mom. He forgot to move them.*

That's when I realized Kordell hadn't followed me into his condo. He was frozen at the door.

"These are from your baby momma," I accused.

"Oh yeah, you know," he confirmed, bumbling through whatever half-truth he was about to tell me. "Brandy was thanking me because I gave her some extra money."

"No, this is bullshit. I'm not dumb," I said, barely raising my voice because I was so dumbfounded. "Don't worry, Kordell, I've figured it out. Thank you for making it so obvious. You're hiding me. You're always talking about her and now here are these flowers. Just admit it! Admit it. You're still in love with her."

I didn't even give him a chance to respond. I walked right out of that condo and had plans of never going back. I broke up with him that night. It was over and it would've stayed over if Kordell wasn't so good at begging.

The old church mothers used to say, "Whoever you spend New Year's with is the person you'll spend the rest of the year with." And

Kordell, even though I was fed up with his lying, wanted to spend it with me. I still wasn't sure I wanted to get back together with him, but because he was so sure and so consistent, it almost overruled my common sense. His confidence in us, in me, hid another little red flag.

So here we were, ten months into our relationship, and he was begging, again, to be with me. I tried to be patient with him because it felt like I had met him in the middle of a process. I had met him in the middle of him trying to get his heart back. I just didn't realize how much of his heart was already spoken for.

Despite his earnest intentions, Kordell didn't spend New Year's with me. When I eventually caught up with him on the other side of a new year, when people are eating their black-eyed peas for good luck and spinach for wealth, and others are going back to the gym for the first time in months, Kordell was catching me up on how he rang in the occasion. Apparently, he had spent the very first night of the year with Brandy and his son. My heart was so worn down by the news, I refused to react. I refused to let his ghosts of relationships past have an effect on me. On us.

"And the next day, I woke up and told Brandy that I wanted to break off the engagement."

"The ENGAGEMENT? Wait. What?!"

"Well, I had proposed to her, and I hadn't really broken it off, and then I met you and then we were moving so fast…"

"So thaaaaat's why you were hiding me. That was your fiancée the entire time!"

"Well, she put the ring on the counter and I took it back so she's not my fiancée anymore."

Even after another flaming red flag that was literally on fire, I threw cold water on the situation because I was in love with Kordell. I ignored the signs about him and his child's mother because I whole-heartedly believed he was my husband.

I knew our story didn't end like this.

So I lied to myself, trying to pretend that this shadow from their relationship wouldn't affect our marriage. Although it did. It always did, because they shared life between them; they had a son together. Because of that, I always felt second rate to her even though I wouldn't dare admit that to him.

So I closed my eyes and ignored the signs about him lying about his engagement. I took him back because I loved him and I really believed once Brandy had given the ring back, he was over her. He said he was.

I stamped out any doubt because I still wanted to marry him. Why would God tell me Kordell was my husband only for it to turn out like this?

After that day, I put the entire situation behind me and it seemed like he did, too. We were in love, in our own little bubble. It felt warm here. It felt safe here. He became my sanctuary.

CHAPTER SIX

"It's ruinnnnned! It's ruinedddddd!" I screamed through hot tears. I didn't want to cry on my wedding day, but here we were. "What am I gonna do?"

"I don't know…" Lauren said honestly, looking at the eight-inch yellow stain on my $25,000 Pnina Tornai ruffled trumpet wedding gown, the very first wedding gown I had ever tried on. I had just taken it out of the protective dust bag and somehow—after transferring it from the bag to my body—it had gotten soiled.

"There's something on my dress!" I said as the bridal suite's butlers came rushing in to see why I was screaming just hours before I was set to walk down the aisle and marry Kordell, the love of my life. "What is it? What is it?"

No one could tell me and no one could calm me down; not even when Lauren told me to "tuck it under, girl, and let's go. You're getting married. It's not like you don't have a second dress for the reception. You'll be fine, girl."

Surely I couldn't get married with a yellow stain on my dress! I hoped, deep down inside, that this would later be a good-luck charm—something I could look back on and laugh about with Kordell on our twentieth wedding anniversary. But fortunately for both of us, after two years of marriage he'd never even hear this story.

"Porsha, this is your wedding day. It's about to happen. It's a stain on your dress, not on your day," Lauren told me in her calming and steady voice.

She was right. This stain wasn't going to ruin my day, especially after what it took to get here.

At twenty-nine years old, I had ignored my gut—that divine intuition trying to protect me from dangers unseen—so many times during our courtship and our engagement that today had to be perfect.

For instance, when Kordell told me that he had used his ex-fiancée's ring to create my emerald-cut engagement ring, I wanted to cut off my finger, it burned so bad from the faux pas. It wasn't even my style.

I remember thinking, *You're actually telling me this? You're admitting that you traded in your ex's ring for mine?* Even though Brandy had given the ring back, there she was again, popping up in the middle of our covenant.

"Yeah, I got a good deal on this ring," he tried to persist, not realizing the gaffe.

"Right! I love it," I lied.

I should've asked Kordell why he would even think to give me someone else's engagement ring, but I couldn't. Even though I was so far from the woman I used to be, and God had given me strength in so many areas of my life, I still wanted to do anything to please him. How could I share my truth if it meant it might hurt the feelings of the person I loved? I hadn't learned yet that holding someone accountable was the very definition of love, but I'd soon learn how to do just that.

I tried to fix it like I always did with things in my life. We spotted this yellow diamond ring in a random jewelry store in Atlanta—that I may or may not have scoped out beforehand—and he bought it for me.

I wish Brandy was the only hurdle we had to clear, but she was just the tip of the iceberg. I had nearly called off everything—the wedding and our relationship. It didn't matter that I had already reserved the venue, and it didn't matter that I had already purchased my dress. Well, two dresses: one for the outdoor terrace ceremony and another for the reception.

Kordell had sprung a prenuptial agreement on me close to the wedding. Without warning or even a prior discussion about it, he had a lawyer draw up the terms and conditions of our marriage. In black-and-white legalese, Kordell made it very clear that he didn't think we were equal partners in our marriage. In legal terms, he saw me more like a housemaid.

You see, Kordell didn't want me to work. He wanted me to sell my business, my daycare, which I did. He wanted me to be a kept woman, and because I really trusted him and thought he had my best interests at heart, I eventually let the daycare go, this business I had built from the ground up. He even wanted to get rid of my penthouse condo, but I had convinced him it was such a great investment that I'd rather just keep it.

As accomplished as I was as a single woman—owning my own home and owning my own business—I didn't hold worth in that. I didn't see the true value in what I had accomplished in my twenties.

Being a wife meant so much more than all of that combined. Being a wife felt like my purpose. It felt like I was born to do it. I was born to embody that role. So when he had asked me to walk away from who I once was, it didn't feel like much of a sacrifice—I believed I was walking into my destiny. My purpose in life was to be his wife. I was walking into God's promise. I was walking into security, into love, into comfort, into care. I believed everything he told me, and it felt like an even exchange.

Not to mention, I wouldn't be walking away from my daycare completely, we decided. Eventually, I had planned to open up another daycare, with Kordell's support, and I did. Sadly, that plan fell through when a developer ran off with $170,000 worth of Kordell's principal investment. So I couldn't blame him when he wanted to hold off on that idea for a while.

But looking at the prenup before we walked down the aisle, it wasn't adding up. So I walked. I never had a problem with walking away from Kordell. I was just terrible at staying away from him.

After our standoff, which lasted a couple of days too long, Kordell told his attorneys to rip the prenup up. Instead of a legal document detailing how he'd provide, Kordell promised that he'd take care of me. I just remember feeling like, *Wow, this man really loves me. He wants to be my partner.*

After all of the prayers, after God told me that Kordell was my husband, I was finally ready to walk down the aisle to become his wife. I was ready to become the woman I knew Kordell wanted me to be. I know that sounds strange to put it that way—that I'd turn into someone else for my marriage. But I wasn't just doing it for Kordell. I was doing it for God.

In finding my spirituality in my late twenties, I went from always wanting to please a man, to wanting to please God. After so many years giving power to men and getting abused, I gave my power to God and found so many joys. My way of being a good wife for God was to be a good, submissive wife. Being submissive to Kordell was number two on my list, behind loving Him. Kordell was the vessel to live out my covenant with God. I knew Kordell would disappoint me with the red flags I had ignored. But I felt that through God, I would find the strength to overcome those disappointments and we'd work through them together. What I didn't realize is that for us to overcome those disappointments, Kordell needed to be equally yoked, so that through his relationship with God, he would never want to betray me. We were speaking two completely different languages, but because the picture looked how we wanted it to look, we went along with it.

Kordell was a good man. He was safe. He was a provider. He was respectable. He was strong willed. He knew what he wanted and he wanted me, he wanted me to be a mother to his son, and to create our own family with our own children. The assuredness, or should I say the vision, that he had for our lives was intoxicating. It was a sheer fairy tale.

Kordell paid for our $3 million wedding. From the wedding planner, to the venue, to my dress—which was made in Florida, so he flew my mom and I back and forth a number of times to get it tailored—to the bridesmaids' dresses, to flying his family in and some of my family into Atlanta to witness our nuptials, to the fireworks at the reception, to our Mexican honeymoon.

I thought that because he wanted me to have the wedding of my dreams, he'd be the man of my dreams.

When you meet someone who can so clearly envision a life for you, it's easy to follow their lead. It's actually comforting because you no longer have to work so hard at life when someone claims to have a blueprint for you—be a kept woman, a modern-day housewife, and a mother. I had won the lottery.

I had always felt that motherhood was my highest calling; that having a child would save my life and give me a deepened purpose that would not only force me to value this life just a little bit more, but also allow me to pour myself so deeply into someone else— growing them while growing myself. Motherhood felt like my priesthood and if Kordell was offering me an easy path to my divine, I felt foolish not to take it.

Becoming a mother to Kordell and Brandy's son was probably the best part of my wedding day. Although I hadn't really spent time with his son before we walked down the aisle, I'll never forget that moment when we were about to take family portraits on our special day. Kordell, looking at his son, said, "You can call her Mom now." From that day on, he called me Mom.

You have to understand, I always longed to be a mom. Especially after having an abortion, it felt like an opportunity to make it right. I couldn't wait to move his son into our home. I couldn't wait to look for his furniture and buy his favorite snacks and take him to practice.

I was so serious about being a great mom to Kordell's son I started going to counseling. Because he was calling me Mommy, I sought professional help because I wanted to make sure I lived up to that title. I didn't know how to fully be a mother because I had become a mom overnight. I hoped going to a family counselor would help me better understand my emotions in my new role as a step-parent, and I encouraged Kordell's son to go as well so he could understand his emotions with suddenly having another mother, especially since his own mother was living in Los Angeles.

It felt like this moment in my life, becoming Kordell's wife and a mother, was ordained. I had lived life. I had overcome my own battles with falling out of love with the essence of life. I had battled losing myself in men and sex and alcohol and work, and when I decided to become a better version of myself, to choose the highest form of myself in order to meet God's vision for me, the very next year I met Kordell.

What I didn't foresee is that the Devil knows God's plans, too, and perhaps I didn't realize that just because something, or rather someone, had the right timing, it doesn't mean it was divine timing. I was just too immature in my faith then to truly discern the difference.

Still, I had unwavering faith. In that moment, I was marrying the man of my dreams—and no prenup and no yellow stain was going to get in my way.

Back in the presidential suite, I took off my wedding dress, handing it over to my bridesmaids, who began working at it, trying to remove the stain as best they could, only to create another stain. Thankfully, Kordell distracted me.

"This is for you," the wedding planner said, handing me a small ring-size box.

Immediately, I knew it was a wedding day gift from Kordell. He had already bought the crystal Christian Louboutins that would carry me to the glass altar, which was surrounded by cascading crystals and flowers. Inside were a pair of diamond earrings. It was the second time I'd cry that day.

A few minutes later, however, the wedding planner came back and handed me another, bigger box. "This is for you...too," she said with a wry smile.

When I opened the second box to see a bracelet that matched the earrings, it felt like confirmation. This day was going to be perfect.

Kordell loved me and after working so hard to create a legacy for myself, it felt nice to choose to be a part of someone else's legacy.

"See? I told you don't let anything ruin your day," my mom said reassuringly, acting as my strength. "Look at these earrings. Look at this bracelet. This is your day to be a wife and to be celebrated."

As night fell on the third-floor terrace of The St. Regis Atlanta on May 21, 2011, my brother Hosea walked me down the aisle in front of about two hundred guests. The stain that we worked so hard to get out had been replaced with a water mark, now conveniently tucked neatly underneath billowing fabric.

I looked around at the guests, sitting on the silver Chiavari chairs, and saw my mother's family, Kordell's former teammates, and so many people in Atlanta who had raised me.

Although my dad wasn't there, we brought a picture of him to the venue so he could see his baby girl marry the man of her dreams.

My mother, on the other hand, was seated right in the front row. I was so enamored with the idea of my wedding day finally becoming a reality and how picture perfect my wedding venue looked through my crystal-dotted veil, complete with a princess-style tiara, that I didn't let my mom's face affect me.

My mom is one of the few people in my life who doesn't have to say anything for me to know exactly what she's thinking. Looking at my mother while holding hands with Kordell, all I saw was a dark cloud over her head, and it stayed there for the entire ceremony. I can always sense whatever energy she's putting out, whether she's trying to hide it or not. But I felt in my heart that she was completely unsure about my marriage. I knew how much it had taken her to offer the encouraging words to me earlier. She was the calm beneath my wings, but that didn't stop her from seeing the train wreck before it happened. But as any parent knows, you have to let the bird fly.

I knew her hesitations and how hard it was to admit them, considering I loved Kordell. Hell, she loved Kordell. We all did.

People always ask, "Why would you ever put up with a controlling man?" Well, they don't start out that way. That's not how a controlling man operates. They have to possess you first. They do that by getting everyone around you to rally for them because then you focus and concentrate on being in love with them.

Kordell always treated me like a princess when we were around my mom and if he treated me like a princess, he treated her like a queen. On Sundays, after we sat side by side, holding hands, listening to my mom preach at church, he wouldn't want to leave my mother's house after Sunday dinner.

My mom had this beautiful yellow couch in her house and after dinner, instead of just cozying up beside me on the couch, he sat on the floor right up under me, rubbing my feet. To the naked eye, it seemed like Kordell worshipped the ground I walked on. And after years of being treated like I was replaceable or so easily discarded, it felt like I had finally found a man who saw me for who I was.

But along with seeing how Kordell cared for me, my mother had also noticed other little things that made her anxious. Of course, like any mother, she didn't tell me her reservations until I left Kordell… the first time. She wanted me to find out for myself.

I wouldn't learn until later that apparently her motherly antenna started to rise when Kordell pushed me to give up my penthouse. Initially, I was okay with that because Kordell had promised we'd build our dream home together. But thanks to my mother's side eye, I decided to hold on to the condo, asking him to cover the $4,000-per-month mortgage instead.

My mother told me later that she also didn't like when he sort of pushed me to buy a new car that I didn't necessarily need.

My car at the time was leaking oil. Now, I had a really beautiful Lincoln SUV, but it was a bit older so it leaked oil sometimes. I know nothing about cars. As long as it takes me from Point A to Point B, I could honestly care less about what goes on under the hood.

But the fact that the truck leaked oil was something that really irritated Kordell to the point where I didn't understand why it was such a big deal. He complained about it so much, he eventually reached his own solution: He'd buy me a new car.

Instead of taking me to the car lot and letting me pick out what I wanted, Kordell bought a car that he loved. Although I felt that Kordell loved and cared for me, even in the most ordinary instances, I struggled to find my voice. I struggled to speak up for myself. I struggled to say, "You know babe, maybe we can get something that's more my style." I didn't want to sound ungrateful or spoiled. So as with my first engagement ring, I just accepted it with a smile.

Still, after we exchanged heartfelt vows, sealed our covenant with God, lit a unity candle under the glass altar, and fireworks went off atop the St. Regis—another surprise to me on my wedding day—my mom was right there helping me back to my hotel room to change into my second wedding dress. This time I slipped into a formfitting corset with a matching skirt to make it easier for Kordell to find and throw my garter. She was right by my side, calming me down, and even leading the family in taking shots of Hennessy.

I told myself that it didn't matter how anyone else felt that day because my wedding was a dream. It was a beautiful day. It was unmatched. It was that beautiful. Even if it was simply the most beautiful fairy tale.

* * *

I should've known that something wasn't right.

After spending a second night in the St. Regis, soaking up every last minute of our fairy-tale wedding, Kordell and I went our separate ways.

"Porsha, I need to go home and grab a few things before we go on our honeymoon. Why don't you go home and grab some things as well?"

It sounded like a good plan to me, especially since we only lived across the street from each other. I felt fine wading my way through the lobby, pressing *P* in the elevator, and waiting patiently for the elevator to reach the top floor to my penthouse condo.

But as soon as I stepped inside my unit, reality had set in. It felt like I had walked into a funeral. I knew that my aunties used to say that when you get married, it's almost like the death of your single life, but it felt like something else was happening here.

It felt like I had walked into a dead person's home. It felt like every part of me was lost and I was literally terrified it'd be gone forever.

What the hell did I just do? What did I just become a part of? I just walked away from everything—my business, this condo? Am I going to be okay? I just up and married this man after only a year and a half! And I'm a mother now?!

I put my hand to my chest to try to steady and calm my breath, which I just couldn't catch. It felt like I couldn't breathe. And because it felt like I was choking, anxiety took over my entire body. Was I going to die the day after I got married? I couldn't breathe. I put my back against the wall and slid down slowly to the floor, crying hysterically. And the tears fell, and fell, and fell hotly onto my cheeks even running down my neck. They wouldn't stop. They wouldn't stop.

Although I knew I was losing who I was in this relationship, I often felt more than happy to give it away. During this moment, however, it felt like the Porsha, my Porsha, that was still happy to be who she was and live how she wanted, was crying out, begging me to see how important she was, how valuable she was, how necessary she was. She didn't want to give up. She didn't want to hide. She didn't want to whisper her real thoughts while saying what he wanted to hear aloud. She wanted to stay.

God, I thought you said this was my husband. Why am I feeling like this? God? God?

When I once felt so close to Him, I could simply close my eyes and hear from Him, this time He felt so far away. I couldn't hear His voice.

So I shook it off.

It felt like a light switch had shut off. That's how easily Kordell changed from being a doting, attentive fiancé to a mean-spirited controlling husband.

It didn't take long to learn who Kordell really was. Although he had made a reputation for himself in the NFL as a player that could excel at any position—running back, wide receiver, quarterback—at home his versatility and willingness to change ended abruptly. It was Kordell's way or the highway.

He told me we were building a home together, but in reality he was building a fortress. He had to approve every single thing we bought for the house: the sheets, the food, the curtains. Being a young wife,

I assumed every wife compromised with her husband and they created a household together. What I didn't realize was that Kordell, in his need to have the final say on every small detail, was going a step further. He controlled what we had in the house, who came into the house, and what they did while they were there.

I mean, if I had guests over and they didn't use a coaster, he'd freak out. And I'd have to spend the next twenty minutes ensuring that there wasn't a ring on the table that he bought.

His high expectations created this atmosphere of unattainable perfection for me as a wife and a mother to his son. I had to be the "Perfect Porsha" in order to avoid his iciness, which cut me deep.

But I tried; I gave it my all because I didn't just commit to Kordell at the altar on my wedding day. I committed to our God-ordained covenant, too, which meant I felt God was at the center of my relationship. So letting this marriage fail would not only be disappointing myself, I felt it might be letting God down as well. I respected the covenant of marriage so much, I would do anything to keep our family together. Because honestly, if it was up to us, I would've left Kordell six months after walking down the aisle. Real talk.

But while I was leaning into trying to be the perfect wife—keeping the house clean, making sure food was on the table, and making sure his son was taken care of—Kordell was always there to remind me that he had bought everything, as if that would make up for everything he lacked. The irony was that if I wanted to, if he had allowed me to keep my daycare, I could've helped support our family, too.

When Kordell bought our house I was thrilled, especially after he revealed it was a wedding present for me to celebrate our love. But what was truly the surprise was that the house that he said was for us didn't have my name on the deed.

I immediately became suspicious because although I was comfortable being a wife, I also thought Kordell saw me as his partner. Leaving my name off of my house's deed felt like a betrayal. Who was he really trying to protect? He was definitely not trying to protect and cover me, which was now his duty as my husband.

While I had an allowance, which was about $1,500 per month, it wasn't enough to cover what I needed to take care of for a house that size and to get his son what he needed, which turned out to be a lot since Kordell—again, without including me in the decision-making process—sued to obtain full custody of his son literally thirty days into our marriage.

Don't get me wrong: A Black man needs to raise his son in this world that will constantly beat him down and disregard him over and over and over again. But you would think a substantial change like that to our household would warrant a deep discussion, which I would've supported. Who doesn't discuss a major decision like that with their new wife?

The way he abruptly ended our honeymoon stage made me question our entire relationship. As much as I loved Kordell, and I knew he loved me, and we had just had the most fairy-tale wedding in all Atlanta, my mind couldn't help but wonder about his ulterior motives—did he marry me to look like a better father?

What I really mean is: Did he only want to get married so he looked more settled and responsible to a family court judge so he could gain full custody of his son, who was really young at the time? Did he get married to have a permanent caretaker for his child so he could continue traveling three times a week and live out his sportscaster dreams?

After Kordell made my entire family fall in love with him—or, more accurately said, made them fall in love with a person he tried so desperately to be—as a way to control me, he began isolating me from my friends and family.

One by one, they all fell victim to some arbitrary rule that Kordell had crafted, and one by one they apparently crossed a line that only he could see. A simple mistake would turn into the entire world crumbling and falling down in Kordell's eyes, and no one could make sense of it. No one could prevent it. We just all had to deal with it.

My aunt talked too much. My girlfriend was too loud. My cousin didn't use coasters. Then my assistant couldn't come over anymore. Next Lauren was banned from the house until eventually nobody was allowed in the house except for me, him, and his son.

Because I was so embarrassed to tell my family and friends, whom I'd known my entire life, that they weren't welcome in my home because my husband was uncomfortable, I just preferred to cut off all communication with them. It was easier for me than having to deal with their likely harmless questions that felt like silver bullets, cracking our picture-perfect façade of a relationship.

I remember when my brother and his kids came over like they always did. By this time Hosea and I had stopped running around the neighborhood and instead his children were running around my house. And soon, if I had it my way, our kids would be running around together. It was something we had always dreamed about, and it was nice having him and his wife so close by so we could see the kids.

Even though the kids were just being kids—running through the house, playing with toys and whatnot—for some reason this visit had sent Kordell over the edge. They had given him even more reason to go off the deep end when they went on a bit of an excursion. Our house sat on a very nice lot of land. Kordell had even bought the lot next door to give us even more space and privacy. Even though there was nothing but grass on our lot next door, Kordell still found a reason to complain: "They left footprints in the grass."

Hosea had had it. He packed up his children and left and I couldn't blame him. He had every right to do that, to protect his family.

That's when I noticed it.

I thought it was just a chill on my feet or the temperature in the house. Everyone always says the first year of marriage is the hardest. I thought it was just a passing phase, something we just had to get through. Or something we had to get used to. I definitely noticed he had changed after we said our vows, but from my experience all men changed after they go from trying to get you to having you. Maybe marriage was just an extreme version of that.

I didn't know what to think, but I knew I could no longer ignore how dark and cold the house felt.

Here we were, embodying the American dream, living in a twenty-thousand-square-foot house that didn't hold any love in any molecule that wafted inside. It was so cold. That house just couldn't get warm, no matter how hard I smiled, no matter what I cooked, no matter what I wore, and no matter what joke I told. That house refused to get warm, especially when he was there.

Everyone says that the first year of marriage is the toughest, but a year into our marriage, it just got worse.

While I was dead set on turning our family of three into a family of four, Kordell wasn't. I hadn't yet caught on to the fact that he was pulling out while I was ovulating, having somehow calculated just when that would be. It didn't occur to me that perhaps something wasn't wrong with me, but instead something was wrong with him, so I made an appointment with a fertility doctor.

At our very first appointment, the doctor told me enthusiastically, "You're pregnant!"

"Whaaaaat! I'm pregnant?!"

"Yes! You are."

"Oh my God!"

I couldn't believe it. I could not believe that after months and months of trying and praying and trying and making deals with God and trying and changing my diet and trying and experimenting with different positions, we had finally gotten pregnant.

I was happy and he seemed happy. He seemed happy that I was happy.

Within the first month of this pregnancy, I started having a lot of abdominal pain. It unnerved me but perhaps, I thought, this is what the body does while carrying a child.

By the second month, Kordell took me to the hospital because the pain had become so severe. I had heard pregnancy was painful, but it never would've occurred to me in a million years that it would be this painful. It didn't seem right. At the hospital, I underwent an ultrasound and the doctors there told me the source of my pain: I had a few fibroids in my uterus, growing at a rapid pace alongside the baby and making my pregnancy high risk. At that time, I didn't even know what fibroids were. Had never even heard of them. I didn't realize just how common they were, especially among Black women.

During the third month, my doctor couldn't find my baby's heartbeat and sent me to a specialist just to make sure. The specialist, thank God, found the baby's heartbeat but also saw a massive fibroid. I was told to be on bedrest for the rest of my pregnancy to mitigate the pain.

I was determined to shrink this fibroid in my womb by any means necessary. I even became vegan because I read that a plant-based diet helps shrink fibroids, but nothing seemed to help. In fact, it felt like the pain was becoming more intense. I could barely get out of bed, let alone walk. I couldn't even go to the bathroom without feeling this intense, sharp pain.

After two more doctors' visits, my specialist told me the news I was dreading: "Your baby still has a heartbeat, but you will have a miscarriage in about two weeks. Because of where your fibroids are located, and because they're not degenerating, your embryo is cornered."

I came home from the doctor's office that day and had to tell my husband the news: My baby, his baby, wasn't going to make it into this life.

When the hard truth fell from my lips, it didn't seem to reach

Kordell. He seemed detached from the pregnancy and detached from me. I didn't feel much support at all, really.

After the first few doctor's visits where I cried in pain, my mom ended up taking me to the rest of the visits and the emergency rooms and the specialists. To this day, I'm not sure if he was so distant because he had never wanted a family with me or because he just didn't know what to say or do. Either way, he wasn't there for me and he left me alone to mourn for our child.

Do you know what torture feels like?

The act of torture—the deliberate, slow, and painful crushing of one's soul and spirit—is telling a woman to go home and try to live her life while carrying a child she knows is not going to make it to the end of the month. How do you get out of bed in the morning? What is the point of brushing your teeth or even combing your hair when the child you're growing inside of you won't have a chance at a life you're absolutely desperate to give them?

About a week or so later, Kordell announced that he was going to a golf tournament. It infuriated me that he could just pick up and go while I stayed here with our child, our dying child, inside me. I begged him to stay. "Why do you need to go right now? Can't this wait? I mean, there will be other tournaments," I said, pleading with my entire womb.

He left anyway.

The very next morning, I started having severe and consistent contractions. I miscarried that day at home, alone, by myself in the guest bathroom.

CHAPTER SEVEN

"Girl, no, never. Definitely not. *Real Housewives* is not for me."

"So you wouldn't be on that show?" my friend Nicki, who just so happened to be friends with a couple of people who produced the reality show, pressed.

"No! I don't know what I would do in those situations with those girls. That drama is crazy," I repeated.

"Weeeell, I kinda already sent your information to some of the producers."

"What?!" I screamed a bit too loudly, not believing what I had just heard.

"Yeaaaah, I told them about you, and how you're a native of Atlanta, and about your grandfather, and you and Kordell are newly-weds, and your philosophy on marriage…and they love who you are and want to talk to you."

I didn't know how to feel. Could I really go through with this? I knew about this show. I was a fan of the show. I knew what this show did for women, either making or breaking them. Honestly, when Nicki first asked me about doing a reality show, I told her there was no way I was signing up for that. I wanted to be an entertainer, like a singer or an actress. I knew I had gifts stirring inside me waiting for the right time and opportunity to be let out. I just didn't see a reality show as part of my plan.

"Porsha! You still there?"

I had been going back and forth, trying to distill if this reality show business was a real thing. Although I still wasn't sure, I just decided to grab the opportunity.

"I mean, okay. I'll talk to them."

Nicki immediately called one of the producers for *Real House-wives* to introduce me. The next thing I knew, I was listening to the producers trying to convince me to film. *Film what?* I thought to myself. I had no idea what people did to create a reality TV show, but from what I gathered from watching Bravo every Sunday night it seemed like a whole lot of fun with a dash of drama on the side.

The producer must've sensed my hesitation so he offered instead: "Well, actually do you have anything coming up? An event or something?"

"Well, I was thinking about planning an event for my family's charity, Hosea Feed the Hungry and Homeless, at my grandfather's house."

"Oh! That'll be great! Do you mind if we come and set cameras up?"

"I don't know because it's a charity event. I'm not really sure... what would you expect me to do?"

"We're just going to bring cameras to your charity event and show the reality. We won't even tell you what to do or say or anything. We're just going to set up cameras."

Well, great! I thought. *This is a great opportunity. I can kill two birds with one stone. I can put my family's charity on this great platform and I can also show what a real young Black marriage looks like and put out that positive image on the show.* I didn't think I'd be anywhere near the drama that I had seen in the previous seasons. I was naive enough to believe I wouldn't get pulled into it. Instead, my goal was to bring this beautiful, positive image of a Black family to the small screen and let people into our world.

The cameras came with a catch, though.

"We're so excited about your event and we want another new cast member to come," a producer, who had called just a few days before the fundraiser, said.

"Oh my God! That would be major," I said.

Now I was excited. I had watched this show every Sunday night—now they wanted me, Porsha Stewart, to film? And I'd be filming with a Black beauty pageant winner?! To me, my new castmate was the ultimate Black representation for little brown girls who looked like me. I was very excited to meet her, but I was also super-nervous, especially since cameras would be rolling.

At the lunch, I tried very hard to get to know her: I asked her how long she had been in Atlanta. What was she doing here? Where was she living? What did she do in her free time? Were we going to spend time together? Looking back on that lunch, I'm sure I was a bit annoying, almost like the little sister who didn't know what to say. Still, I had the best intentions of trying to forge a friendship with her.

But when we met a second time, a simple slip of the tongue would get our burgeoning relationship off to a rocky start. I didn't realize that by the end of my charity event I'd be walking down to the end of my grandfather's driveway in East Lake trying to convince this woman to come back inside and failing miserably, despite my best efforts. I didn't even realize I had cut her so deeply until she stormed out of my grandfather's home.

Luckily, Kordell had already left the charity event by that point. Because if he knew what had happened, he would've shut it down.

It had already taken some convincing for my then-husband, who desperately valued his privacy, to warm to the idea of opening our young marriage up to the world. In fact, his first two words when I told him that *Real Housewives* cameras were coming to film the event were, "Oh no."

He went on, "That show is crazy—"

"Listen, listen, listen, Kordell, we have a great opportunity," I said, cutting him off and starting my spiel. "I'm a quintessential housewife and you're an ex-athlete.

"It'll be a great way to show off your beautiful life and how you've pivoted into having a thriving TV career," I continued, hinting at his ESPN gig, where he was a sports commentator at the time.

"Look at us, we're married. We're raising a young Black son. We can be that young blended family, showing how you can be successful and grow together," I told him after that fateful phone call with the producers. "This is what the world needs to see. We can show that we're a power couple."

Although we both knew that our marriage was having issues, so many issues, we were used to pretending that everything was all right, or at least believing that everything was going to be all right. With the issues we were having, I knew I needed a life outside of our marriage. He wasn't allowing me to work—even charity events counted toward "work" in his mind—he just wanted me to take care of him and his son. At first, I wanted that life, but when I realized I didn't have any of my own money, I knew I needed something for myself. I wanted to show our young Black family to America, but I also knew I needed something of my own as a young Black woman.

I wasn't worried about bringing our marriage to reality TV and, thankfully for me, he wasn't, either.

"And to kick it off, I'm going to do a charity event!"

"All right, I love that. I love that. That sounds cool," he said, warming up to the idea, especially when it came with crafting the picture-perfect narrative.

When I needed him this time, Kordell was there for me. He didn't say a word when I shelled out $60,000 to plan a last-minute charity event. I had rented a white tent and beautiful furniture to hold a catered dinner—complete with uplighting, place settings, centerpieces, and gifts—where we'd be serenaded by a band.

Before I left our house, wearing a strappy gold dress with my hair swept up, Kordell even gave me a pep talk when he sensed I was a bit nervous. He asked me, "Baby, do you have everything you need? I want this to be your moment so I'm not going to be there tonight.

I want you and your girls to just enjoy the night. I hope you raise a lot of money."

After all that we had been through recently with losing the baby, his support meant the world to me. It felt like we were finally back on the same wavelength after feeling out of sorts for weeks. Perhaps this show would be the shared vision we needed to keep our relationship intact.

By the time the cameras had arrived, I thought to myself, *This is fabulous!* I was living in the moment and loving every second of it. The attendees, dressed in their cocktail attire, were filing in and sitting at the tables I'd specially designed for the evening.

Fifty or so people from the production crew showed up to my grandfather's house, turning my ordinary charity event into one that was going to be streamed to millions of viewers. It changed the event in so many ways.

There were cameras everywhere, it seemed, in each corner of the room and some floating about. The crew had also installed additional lighting down his driveway and inside the actual tent where the dinner was being held. Although I had bought and paid for a band for the evening, we couldn't really play any music because it would've made it hard for editors to slice the scenes together later.

It didn't feel like I was filming a reality TV show at all, which surprised me. In fact, the only thing producers told me before the event started was, "Just go ahead with the night. There's nothing that we need you to do or need you to say. We're just here to follow your reality."

Even though I didn't have to do anything, I still felt reaaaally, reaaaaally nervous because not only was I hosting an event in front of every woman that I cared about, but it was also in front of the cameras. I was so careful about every blink, every walk, every hug, every smile. I wanted to be picture perfect.

Not only was I not used to being in the center of a camera, my friends and family weren't used to it, either. So there we were, on our best behavior, trying to suck in, smile, and make sure the cameras caught our best angles.

Somehow Kordell knew just what to do to make me look good for the show. He surprised me by popping up at the event and presenting me with a custom cake and a gift, a beautiful black Chanel bag, while cameras captured his benevolence. He didn't stay long, though, wanting it to truly be my night. Thankfully Kordell left before the entire charity event dissolved, with cameras rolling, leaving me to deal with my new castmate alone.

This night was meant to honor her and welcome her to Atlanta. I even had an award created for her. Standing in front of the band and the cameras, I made a speech to welcome the guests, sharing how important it was that we as women gathered to raise money to pour back into our communities. I also wanted to use the opportunity to present this beauty queen with the award.

"I just want to announce that we do have Miss America here…" I said to the women in attendance.

It was a total Freudian slip. My castmate's immediate side eye let me know that I had gotten her title wrong; she was actually Miss USA. When I saw her face, I immediately said, "I'm sorry!" and continued on with the speech, hoping she would be forgiving of the slip.

Although I had moved on from the mistake pretty quickly to save face, in my mind I was soooo embarrassed. I could've died that I messed up her title. I could've literally folded into myself like a roly-poly and just rolled behind the band. It's just that I was so nervous, I didn't know what was coming out of my mouth.

I eventually sat down at the table we were sharing and apologized again, but then I realized, *Oh, wow. She's not even accepting my apology.* She really copped a whole attitude. Her entire energy had shifted and for the rest of the night she kept looking at her phone almost as if she wanted to leave. Eventually, she did in fact leave.

I didn't know who else to turn to so I pulled a member of the production aside. I was frantic, trying to look like I had it together.

While I loved the cameras initially for the platform they could provide for my charity event, now I wanted to smash all of them in a million pieces so they couldn't capture what was happening.

"Oh my God. What am I supposed to do? Let's cut the cameras because this isn't going the way it's supposed to go."

"What do you mean? We're here to film your reality. Go on and tell her what you want her to know."

It still didn't register to me what I was supposed to do while cameras were detailing my every move. So I asked, "What do you mean? I want her to come back in and sit down."

"Well go tell her that," one crew member advised.

But this wasn't supposed to go like this. This was my first time filming for the show and it was turning into a horror show. How did I end up in such a misunderstanding and why couldn't I calm this woman down? I'm human. I'm used to making mistakes and then saying, *My bad, I apologize. That's not what I meant.* For some reason, though, she just wouldn't let it go. I was completely thrown off. I was completely confused.

That's when I realized: While I was trying to calm down a guest at a charity event meant to continue my father's legacy and raise money for the community, she was literally making a scene.

What I didn't realize was that this particular cast member had already filmed a lot for the show by the time she showed up to my charity event. Not to mention, she was in music videos and had done some acting. She knew what she was doing.

I, on the other hand, had never been in front of these types of cameras. Every time a camera pointed in my direction, I felt my heart race and my breath quicken and my palms sweat while I sat there trying to be natural. I was low key—well, really, high key, freaking out. It caused me to say a lot of dumb things, especially while filming my first season, that I simply didn't realize or mean.

After realizing that she was doing what I like to call "Housewives stuff," it made me freak out even more because that's not why I had joined the show. I honestly wanted no part in the drama. I didn't know where she was going to take it and if she had planned to take down my family legacy right along with her.

What fans didn't see because it happened off camera was that a producer came to me as she was huffing and puffing out the door and said, "So, she's leaving and she wants a plate of food to go."

"A plate to go?!"

It was one thing to want to leave my charity event because of an offense and an entirely different thing to demand a to-go plate. The audacity was baffling to me. Let's just say, she never got that plate of food to go.

Standing at the foot of the driveway of my family home, she continued to blow the fact that I had referred to her as Miss America instead of Miss USA way out of proportion, even calling me "disrespectful." So I had no choice but to ask her to leave.

When I got home that night, taking off one gold shoe after the other, I thought I had blown it. I thought I had gone on camera and made a complete fool out of myself. I thought I was a nervous and bumbling mess. I thought I'd never hear from producers again.

But the next thing I knew, Kordell and I were being invited to Anguilla to film again and I couldn't be more excited.

I didn't quite realize what I was getting Kordell, his son, and I into when I invited cameras into the family home that I grew up in. I didn't quite realize how much I'd be sacrificing when those cameras began rolling. I didn't quite realize how tough I'd have to become when it all began. It didn't hit me until I watched my first season, season five, as it rolled out episode by episode on Bravo.

I saw myself in a whole new way, in an entirely different world, when I watched myself on TV. I saw my reactions to the other women. I saw some of the dumb stuff I said. I saw how my marriage looked on TV. I saw how I looked on TV, which was nothing like the confident, compassionate, funny woman I knew, and I said to myself, *I've just made a huge mistake. We look terrible. I really don't know if I can go through with this.* Watching this different version of myself on TV felt like I was swimming in a great big blue ocean, but unable to catch my breath with no life jacket or shore in sight.

It didn't help that I was so new to social media. In fact, I had literally just joined Instagram a few weeks after I had started filming the show. I was used to my girls writing comments underneath my squared photos, saying, "Oh, you're so fab. You look great!" "That food looks good." "Congratulations to you and your husband." So when those comments turned more critical, and at some points downright rude, I wasn't prepared at all. Every person's comment that I read felt as if they were saying it straight to my face; and they were fighting words at that. Even though I often didn't know the people behind these hurtful tweets and Instagram comments, their typed words cut deep and stayed with me long after I had stopped scrolling. It was a shock to my system—an emotional shock—shaking the very core of who I was or who I thought I was portraying.

In front of those cameras, I thought I was presenting an ambitious young woman who lived in Atlanta and had an inspiring family that had done a lot for the community. I thought viewers would see a Black woman with a loving and caring husband. The picture that I was painting was beautiful to me. But it wasn't until I read those social media comments that I realized people were watching someone completely different.

The cameras couldn't hide my insecurities. They couldn't hide my anxiety. They couldn't hide how nervous I was to be in front of those little black lenses. Growing up when I used to stare at my mother's camcorder, creating my own TV show through similar-looking lenses, it didn't feel like this. The people I imagined watching me at that age thought I was smart, beautiful, and talented. What was even better was that my imaginary audience understood me and my sense of humor and my heart. These viewers, whom I was just getting to know, didn't see that yet.

What made it even trickier was that Kordell didn't want cameras taking up space between us in our home. So when it was time to film, Nene Leakes and Cynthia Bailey came to the Hosea home, the same place where I had hosted the charity event. I had planned to discuss Hosea Feed the Hungry and Homeless while Nene updated us on her Twisted Hearts Foundation, which aimed to help victims of domestic violence. Meanwhile, Cynthia was just about to launch The Bailey Agency, which helped give aspiring models more visibility.

I couldn't camouflage how excited I was to welcome Nene and Cynthia into my family's home. These were the same women I had watched Sunday after Sunday on my own television. It's why I'd make senseless gaffes that I never would've made if I was just simply living my life without millions of people potentially watching.

My heart began racing as I watched the *Real Housewives* OG, the woman who literally started the show, and her model best friend Cynthia step out of a white Range Rover. When the ladies showed up to film that day, with those cameras in tow planning to capture our every move and facial expression, I clammed up a bit.

I had never met these ladies before so I wasn't sure what to expect. I didn't know if they'd be nice, if they'd be mean, if once the cameras turned on they'd be hilarious and then once the cameras turned off they'd curse me out. I had no clue so I just said a silent prayer and hoped for the best. If you watch that episode in season five, you can hear Nene say, "Nice to meet you," when I opened the door to my grandfather's home because we hadn't really met until then.

I was so excited to talk about Hosea Feed the Hungry and Homeless. I remembered thinking, *Make sure you get the facts straight because this is your family's charity, this is your family legacy.* The last thing I wanted to do while millions of people were watching was mess up how they could support us.

While on the outside I may have looked like I had it all together, inside I felt so nervous that I let my words fly out of my mouth. It almost felt like I couldn't control them, slipping out in ways that I wasn't used to. I was used to being the Porsha who spoke in church pulpits and knew what to do on the mic. I knew how to string words together so well, I felt I could preach the Gospel and minister to people and bring them closer to God. So it didn't make sense that once cameras turned to me, words felt like they were slipping through the palms of my hands and all I could do was watch as gravity pulled them to the ground, scattering them.

I was telling Nene and Cynthia that the charity, which feeds thousands in need, didn't just operate on Thanksgiving Day. This was something my family had emphasized to me—I had to share that our mission took place year-round. We really did the work every day. I had so much adrenaline running through me as I connected with these women, who had told me they were familiar with our charity work, and I was so nervous and excited to get the words out, that I said, "265 days a year," and I didn't even flinch when I said it. I didn't even catch myself. I didn't even realize I had said "265" instead of "365." It was so embarrassing, oh my God.

I watched in my bedroom by myself months later when the episode aired. At first, I thought, *Wow I look so confident, I am really representing my family well.* When the words came out my mouth, I had to rewind the tape to confirm I had made the mistake.

After that now-iconic episode aired, I was bombarded by hurtful messages on social media. Some were calling me "dumb," others were saying I was "a disgrace," asking, "Where did this girl come from?" I felt so crushed because a true slip of the tongue caused people to seriously question my intelligence, my character, and who I was.

It really did hurt my feelings. It hurt so bad that I broke down, crying hysterically to Nene and Cynthia on a three-way call, screaming "I can't do this! I don't want to do this anymore. What is happening? People don't like me. People are calling me names. People are being downright cruel."

The ladies knew what it felt like to be misunderstood by the viewers, and the bloggers, and the media. They understood what it meant to be unhappy with the way you were portrayed or just from talking too much or not enough. They told me that it was okay to feel how I was feeling, especially when it came to how my marriage looked on TV, but to quickly get over it.

"It's okaaaaay," Nene advised. "It's your first season. Everybody goes through this first season."

"She's right," Cynthia added. "Everybody goes through this, but Porsha, you're built for this. You can do this. That's why they picked you! You know how many women would kill for this job? They chose you for a reason."

Nene and Cynthia literally had to talk me out of leaving the show that day because of the online harassment, and I'm thankful they did. In fact, it always seemed that Nene, in particular, was there to either calm me down or give me true tea throughout the ups and downs of my first season.

"You know you and Kordell gon' break up, right?" she told me during one of those conversations.

"Excuse me?!" I said, completely offended by the suggestion. I didn't care who she was; she wasn't gonna sit here and tear down my marriage.

"No. Seriously. I don't mean any harm, but the show is going to change your marriage. Mark my words. I'm not telling you what I heard. I'm telling you what I know, Porsha. Now, listen to me," she said in that signature Nene twang that I had fallen in love with during season one of *Real Housewives*.

"You on this TV show, right? Their pussy game go up. You know how these women be," Nene said of those kinds of women who throw themselves at any man they see on TV. "And in the meantime while he's at work and while he's at the grocery store and while he's with his boys, people are calling him 'Porsha's husband.' It doesn't matter what job he has now: Because he's no longer on that field, he's losing fame, and now you're the star. He ain't gon' like that and he ain't gon' like you having all this time dedicated to something outside of the house."

I didn't want to believe it, but every single warning Nene uttered that day came to fruition.

I thought the cameras would be a good distraction from the very real problems we were facing in our marriage, but they weren't distracting at all. If anything, they magnified the façade we had built brick by unsteady brick.

I had oddly gotten used to Kordell's controlling behavior, but then he stopped coming home. Because of his job, he'd only be in our home for three days out of the week anyway, but when he began not even coming home for those three days and not answering his phone late at night when I called, I knew something was up. Especially because when I texted that I was calling about his son, he'd call back immediately, but he refused to answer my calls any other time.

With Kordell, it was a mental game. He seemed to want to control every single thing about my life: how much money I had, where I lived, what I wore, who came into our home. But when it came to reaching him, accessing him, or letting me into his life, I could never reach him. Even though I was his wife, I couldn't get through to him. It was infuriatingly frustrating. Every unanswered call slowly killed my spirit, my confidence, and my common sense. It was like he wanted me to second-guess myself and become solely dependent on his whim.

I was willing to fight for my marriage, for our marriage. I knew men cheated. Hell, my daddy cheated. I could forgive that, but what I wasn't willing to do was actually fight.

I'll never forget the day everything changed.

As part of the control he had over me, I was completely isolated from family and friends. Because he said who stayed and who went, nobody came over. Our house was cold, unfriendly, and unwelcoming on purpose. For a person who longs to have her village hang out inside her home all the time, it was literally crushing me to be alone in that big old house.

So one night, even though it was a rare night when he was actually home, I decided, *You know what? I'm going out with my friends.*

I'm going out. I don't care what Kordell says. When I crawled into our bed around 2:00 a.m., I knew I was going to pay for it. I eventually woke up later that morning to Kordell, who was already up. Of course. Instead of hearing my alarm clock, I heard his voice yelling:

"You're sleeping all day because you've been out all night! You didn't even cook breakfast!"

"What?" I said, trying to open my eyes to a brand-new day. "Kordell, please, I'm tired! I went out last night. That's what happens when you go out late, you sleep in late."

That day we had an argument that was worse than any we had had up until that point. What he said and did was unforgiveable. While there is more to this story I can't share for legal reasons, I knew it was the beginning of the end.

"I'm leaving you."

I didn't hesitate to make good on my words. I got in my car and sped off to my mom's house. But I didn't dare tell my momma what had just happened. She'd kill him.

Although this was the first time I said those words—"I'm leaving you"—to Kordell, it wouldn't be the last.

Kordell begged me to come back. He pressed me. He pleaded with me. I told Kordell I'd come back to our home, to our marriage, if he took care of some assurances that I needed in the marriage. I wanted him to go to weekly couples therapy. I wanted my name on the deed of our house because it was our family home. I also wanted health insurance. For the past couple of years, I couldn't even take myself or his son to the doctor if we needed to go. I didn't even have the basics to survive.

We had barely made it to our two-year anniversary before we got into another argument over something I can't even remember—maybe he didn't like something I said, maybe he got sick of me asking for grocery money, or maybe I didn't clean the bathrooms the right way. Who the hell knows, but Kordell got so upset one night that I said, "I'm leaving and I'm leaving you."

"No, Porsha, you're not," he said in a tone that was so matter-of-fact it scared me.

Thank God his son was asleep already because Kordell proceeded to chase me around the house, trying to lock every single door so I couldn't leave. I ran to one of the doors as fast as I could, but the knob wouldn't turn. I jangled it as hard as I could, but it wouldn't budge. I was locked inside. Again.

A terror and a rage filled my entire body. I would not be confined one more time.

"I'm leaving!" I screamed from the other side.

My eyes darted to a bottle of prescription pills that just so happened to be in the room. I grabbed the bottle from the table and shakily screwed off the top. Taking a sip of water, I swallowed six or so pills. It wasn't the whole bottle, but it was enough to get me out of this house.

By the time Kordell had finally opened the door, I was out of it.

"What the fuck are you doing? This is crazy. I can't believe you did this," he said, screaming at me.

I was laid out on the floor, barely conscious, but I had enough strength to say, "Call 911 because I'm leaving here one way or another."

CHAPTER EIGHT

I had gotten used to waking up alone.

It had nothing to do with Kordell always traveling for his on-air gig, or traveling to weekend golf trips, or traveling to God knows where with his boys.

While I never caught him red-handed stepping out on our marriage—aside from seeing text messages on his phone, asking his baby momma to "send me a picture of that pussy" only four months after walking down the aisle—a woman always knows something is up.

Thank God for women's intuition, that blessed knowledge in your gut that tells you something ain't right. The feeling as the hairs on the back of your neck rise when you can't help but notice that something doesn't quite add up. Or perhaps it's my ancestors warning me from yesteryears of their own heartbreaks, but I could always tell when he was lying and sometimes for my own pride, I'd wished he'd be better at it.

I couldn't stand sleeping in the same bedroom as my husband anymore. There was one night in particular I suggested I sleep in a different bed, and he refused to let me go. He insisted we sleep in the marital bed together. He was dead set on me continuing to play this role. By not sharing a bed with him, even with all our issues, in his eyes that meant I wasn't fulfilling my duty.

I landed on the bed while I continuously told him, pleaded with him, "No, no, no!" I remember looking into his eyes and recognizing that familiarity of seeing no soul there. I just remember seeing that same darkness on his face that I saw on Southern Jon. I couldn't believe that I had married that face; that this was the man I committed my life to, this was my husband who I had never cheated on or taken for granted, and was now abusing me.

So while our master bedroom sat on the first level, overlooking our beautiful uplit pool, I packed up my nightstand and moved to an upstairs bedroom. If I couldn't find peace in my bed, I was going to create peace in my home.

Of course that angered Kordell. What didn't anger Kordell?

Out of what seemed like retaliation, Kordell had his brother stay with us for extended periods of time. So now here I was, a young woman, living with two grown men. During his visits, I rarely left my bedroom because I didn't want to bump into them around the house. It wasn't right. It didn't feel right. It wasn't long before I had asked my sister, Lauren, to come over to the house regularly until I figured out when and how this standoff would end. Her presence made me feel more comfortable in my own home.

I rolled over in my bed that March morning, my body waking

with the day. Instead of reaching out for Kordell, as I would have during happier times, I reached for my cell phone. I was actually relieved.

I did my usual morning routine—made sure my scarf was still in place, did a light stretch down through my toes, and checked my text messages. I didn't see any that needed to be answered right away so I moved on to the weather app. It looked like another sunny day in Atlanta. And then I checked Twitter.

Despite all the confusion, mess, and sadness that kept lingering around me, taking up space inside my home, hope pierced through my spirit this morning. So I tweeted a prophetic phrase: "Today is the first day of the rest of your life."

I rolled back over, falling headfirst into my plush guest bed. By the time my body naturally woke back up, a few hours later, I had dozens of random text messages and several missed calls from Lauren. Apparently, she had called me back-to-back-to-back-to-back. Something was wrong.

I clicked on Lauren's name and she answered on the first ring: "Have you heard?"

"Heard what?"

While she tried to come up with the words to tell me that I was getting divorced and I was the very last person to know, I clicked Twitter to see what she was talking about. My stomach dropped when I realized I was one of today's Trending Topics and it wasn't even Sunday—the day when my name usually trends on Twitter as *The Real Housewives of Atlanta* airs on Bravo.

Then I read a headline I will never forget: "Kordell Stewart Is Divorcing Real Housewives Star Porsha Stewart."

I felt my stomach drop immediately as if I was riding a roller coaster at Six Flags. *Kordell is divorcing me? Kordell is divorcing me?!* I kept reading and rereading the headline over and over, trying to make it make sense, but it didn't.

I mean, I was the one who had asked for a divorce after Kordell stole all that he could from me and he refused. He told me coldly that "if you want a divorce, you're going to have to file," knowing I couldn't afford to do it. *With what money?!*

Kordell was downstairs. I couldn't believe this man didn't even have the courage to tell me our marriage was officially over. I had to find out that he had filed for divorce from Twitter. The world found out I was divorcing a man that I had sacrificed so much for before he had the decency to let me in on it. He couldn't even text me to give me a heads-up like, "Hey. Didn't want to wake you, but I filed for divorce. See you in the kitchen." But no. Instead, he waited for me to come to him. Yet another power play from the master manipulator.

"Did you file for divorce?" I asked matter-of-factly, skipping the morning pleasantries yet trying hard not to start an argument first thing in the morning. "You could've told me."

"Well, I thought about it," he claimed, before rushing out: "Let's talk about it later."

Kordell then got up, grabbed his bag, and walked past me out of the room, leaving me standing there with even more questions.

When my husband—well, estranged husband—wouldn't give me answers, I asked another man: my attorney. I called and asked him to look up whether there were any court documents filed from Kordell, and sure enough, without even much digging, my attorney found that Kordell had filed for divorce in Georgia's Fulton County Superior Court.

Immediately my mind turned to my survival. Although I was now getting a check from Bravo for becoming a fan favorite on *Housewives*, when I learned that Kordell had actually filed, my first thought was *Oh my God, they're going to fire me for getting a divorce*.

After happily and lovingly giving that man every single thing he asked for, including putting our family first, I finally chose something for me—something that would give me financial success and broaden my sense of purpose. Now he was trying to rip it away from me.

If I'm being honest with myself, I signed up for *The Real Housewives of Atlanta* to impress Kordell. A small part of me convinced him to do the show so that he could look at me the way that he used to look at me. I wanted him to think highly of me. I wanted him to say, *Wow! Look at my wife. She's doing it!* I wanted him to respect me, and if I couldn't get respect in my household, I thought maybe if I was respected by other people, he would respect me, too.

When I walked down the aisle to Kordell, I thought I was going to be his partner. I thought I was going to be the person that he admired, looked to, confided in. I thought he would have that light in his eye when he looked at me. But once I became his wife, it started to vanish. I had become a housekeeper. I had become a nanny. I had become simply his wife. I didn't feel seen. I didn't feel heard. I didn't feel important. I didn't feel valued.

I wanted *Housewives* to give me respect in my marriage. What I didn't know was that it was going to intimidate him, make him jealous, and eventually make him pull away.

Early in our marriage, especially when we were in a nice part of town, we'd often hear Kordell's name being called.

"Oh, Kordell! Kordeeeeeell!"

He always hesitated when hearing his name called and eventually stopped to say hi, take pictures, and sign autographs. Even on days when my feet hurt and I just wanted to sit down; even on days when I was cramping and just wanted to sleep in our bed; even when I didn't want to be bothered, we stopped. And I didn't mind stopping because that's what an athlete's wife is supposed to do: stop, smile prettily, and offer to take their picture.

As the episodes kept airing on Bravo, though, people would be stopping us, but not to talk to Kordell. They'd be stopping to talk to me. *Housewives* fans, especially girls from the A, when they'd see me, they wouldn't just be polite and yell my name. They'd show love! They'd stop. They'd chat. They'd catch up, take pictures, and hold my hand until they were done talking to me so I couldn't slip away.

Kordell did not like that. In fact, after one run-in, I distinctly remember him telling me, "There's only one star in this house!"

I sensed that he especially didn't like how the camera saw the real him, the one he couldn't cover up with charm—and he did have a lot of it. It's one of the reasons why I fell so much in love with him. Sadly for us, fans let us both know that they didn't like it, either. As much as he wanted to blame editing for how he appeared on TV, the reality is that even if sometimes editors would do a bit of light editing, editors couldn't make up the words that came out of his mouth. They couldn't use "movie magic" to create his on-screen image. His controlling personality came out on camera and, you guessed it, he blamed me for it. He blamed me for how he was perceived on television, which made no sense.

Our divorce was obviously a long time coming. When he rarely came home anymore, I knew Kordell had checked out, but I still tried to hold on tightly to our marriage with both hands, even if my hands were burning and my knuckles were bleeding. I did it with pleasure.

Because I felt, and truly believed, that this marriage was not just between me and him. It was between him, me, and God, you know? So it didn't matter what he was doing or what he wasn't doing because I wasn't just in the marriage with him. As much as I was fine with letting Kordell down, letting God down felt wholly and completely different.

Even when he would be out of town and wouldn't answer the phone and leave me hanging, I would just take it to God in prayer. I'd ask God, *Listen, my husband is acting up, but God, I'm in this. I'm in this marriage and I made a promise to you so I'm going to keep trying. Please help me, God, because I'm tired of trying by myself. I'm tired; so, so tired. Give me strength.*

I had always wanted to speak life into Kordell. It was especially important for me as his partner because when we first met he almost looked like a broken-winged bird to me. He was a recluse, a total introvert. Kordell felt his career as a quarterback with the Pittsburgh Steelers was stolen by rumors of him being a closeted gay man, which I didn't believe were true, but they refused to go away. Unfortunately, with the culture of the NFL being what it was at the time, he felt these rumors led to an early end to his career. It was truly a heartbreaking story because Kordell felt robbed of his favorite thing in the world and of his life's purpose. He felt like these rumors ruined his entire career.

Because of that pain, being tortured by a passion you can no longer pursue because of what he felt were baseless lies, he became completely disinterested in people. He could no longer trust them. He couldn't. So Kordell wouldn't go anywhere. He would golf 24/7. Even that night at the club, when we met, he was forced to go out because it was one of his homeboy's birthdays, but he didn't want to be there, either. Fate truly brought us together that night.

I'm the one who brought him around family and friends and church and community because it was heartbreaking to watch him struggle with losing a career that I knew, and he knew, he had been born to do and that he had worked so hard to have. It was hurtful realizing that he had been through that kind of pain.

I loved him and my family felt the same. We got to know Kordell for who he was and I think he really needed that; his soul really needed that. Because once we got to know him, Kordell became such a vibrant, outgoing, and cool person.

But right now, in this moment, after reading that headline, I couldn't help but feel like I had been duped by the entire relationship.

I didn't have anywhere to go when Kordell decided that he didn't want to be married anymore. Thankfully, the constant in my life—my mother—urged me to move in with her while I figured out my next move. We just didn't know how hard that was going to be…for both of us.

I didn't realize I'd never step foot back inside that house again. Kordell couldn't wait two weeks to push me out of the house I desperately tried to make a home. He called a moving company to pack my stuff up and put it all boxes and drop it at my momma's house. I couldn't believe that he had stuffed my entire life—my clothes, my belongings, my memories—into cardboard boxes.

I even had to fight back tears once I realized that on every check he had ever given me he had written the word *loan* on the bottom of it to make it clear that everything between us was separate. I didn't notice any of this until I started contemplating getting a divorce.

My mother always worried something would happen to me in that house. Of course she didn't tell me at the time, but she spent a lot of time talking to God, asking Him to cover me from Kordell, so she was just glad to have me back home.

Although real life was smacking me around, it's not like I could tell the cameras to stop rolling, especially during the realest moments of my life. Truly Original, the production company behind *The Real Housewives of Atlanta*, wanted to film my fall from grace, as humiliating as it was. Because I had signed my name on that dotted line, I had to agree to let millions of people watch how I failed at something I wanted to work so desperately. I could only imagine what viewers would think of me, watching me pick up the pieces of my life in my momma's home after seeing my marriage fall apart.

What does it say about me when I'm a housewife on *The Real Housewives* and can't hold down my home? What does that say about me as a woman? I lost my husband, my home, my identity, my business, and now I was about to lose my show. It didn't feel fair that I'd have to sacrifice so much of myself for marriage.

With rumors that the producers were thinking of giving me the ax now that I was divorced, I just gave in. Even though I was only letting cameras inside my momma's home, I was also letting cameras take my dignity and pride.

Bravo wanted to film me moving back into my mother's house after I was essentially kicked out. Initially, I had moved my suitcases into one of my mother's smaller bedrooms and my mom and I watched as the camera guys zoomed in on my suitcases as one by one the movers brought my boxes in.

On a show like *Real Housewives*—well no, let me be more accurate: On a franchise like *Real Housewives*, where women get divorced and move into their summer home in Hawaii or the Hamptons—I knew what it looked like when this little Black girl was moving back to her mother's house on the other side of Atlanta. Overwhelmed by it all and how it might affect my standing on the show, my mother stepped in to protect me, or at least protect my dignity. If you've ever scrolled down the #RHOA timeline on Sunday night, you know just how amazing our fans can be, but also how their truth and honesty can cut you deep, especially when you're already hemorrhaging.

"Isn't Porsha moving into the guest bedroom?" the producers asked, pointing to a smaller bedroom in the house. "Wouldn't she naturally be putting her things into that room?"

"No, no, no, hell no. Porsha, tell the movers to bring your stuff and put it in my bedroom," my mom replied, waving her lacquered fingernail toward the three men who held my belongings and pointing to her master bedroom upstairs.

"Y'all want her to be filmed moving back, right? Well you ain't gon' be showing her packing her stuff into one of the tiny rooms in the house and looking all sad because she's getting divorced...no. She's moving into my room."

After fighting with Kordell, I didn't have any more fight left in me. I spent the past few months fighting for the bare minimum: fighting for health insurance that he promised me, fighting for him to hear my voice, fighting for my house to feel like a home again, fighting to feel like the decisions I made for his son were honored and respected.

I even fought for my safety from a man who swore—no, he vowed—to honor and cherish me. I just couldn't muster up enough strength to fight with producers about filming my own life. Thankfully, when my voice had no power left in it, my mother gave voice to me.

"Listen, this is our reality. She's not going to one of the other bedrooms. She's going to take my bedroom because her spirits need to be up," my mother said matter-of-factly, standing her ground, her hands power-posing on her hips.

"But Ms. Dianeeee," the producer said exasperated, looking away, then down, clearly losing this fight, "where's your bedroom going to be then?"

"All the goddamn bedrooms are my bedrooms. So Porsha is going to be in this one," she said, pointing upstairs to the master.

One of the cameramen, confused about what they should be pointing their lenses to next, asked the producer what the call was, but my mother responded instead.

"No, we're not going to film her moving her suitcases into that bedroom," she said, looking straight at him. "If you don't film this, you won't be filming anything because her things aren't going into the other room."

Next thing I knew, cameramen followed me upstairs, pulling my suitcases across the catwalk and into the master.

What cameras didn't capture, thankfully, was that soon after I had moved back in, my mother was evicted from her own home. She knew it was coming because she was trying to fight the eviction in court, but she couldn't stop it. They showed up at my mother's house anyway and started carrying her belongings out onto the front lawn for all the neighbors to see.

My mother losing her home didn't only affect her. It meant that we were both out of a place to live, along with my mom's mother and husband, who were also staying with her at the time. They were put out, too.

I just remember getting a call from my mother, telling me not to come anywhere near her house because she was being put out and all her stuff was now sitting on the front lawn.

This was after my first season of *Real Housewives* had already aired. People were already stopping me in the streets, in the grocery store, taking pictures of me without my permission, and honking their horns to see if I would turn my head. And I guess my mother didn't want my name being dragged through the blogs any more than it already was thanks to Kordell. She didn't want anyone to know that we were now homeless. It was our little secret.

I took what was left of my check from *Housewives* and found a nice hotel to stay in for two weeks after putting all our stuff in storage. It was me, my mother, my grandmother, and her husband all in two hotel rooms.

I tried anything to avoid the inevitable, to avoid being homeless, even asking a friend for help. This was the same friend who wanted all my time, wanted me to stay on the phone, wanted me to travel with him, but he refused to help me at one of my lowest points in life.

It was a good reminder for me that you really can't depend on anybody except yourself. Nobody ever gave me anything. I've had to fight my way to and fight my way through every obstacle and setback and challenge in my life. I only had my mom. I only had my family. We only had us. We always had to figure it out on our own. We never got bailed out.

God tested our faith. He never just sent someone who said, *Boom! Here you go. Here's some money to make this problem go away.* (Although that would've been really, really nice, God.) Instead, he gave a situation where we'd have to depend on Him, grow in our faith, and come out better on the other side of it. He never failed us.

Even though it was a really hard time, that was one of the most fun times I've ever had with my family. We used to be in the hotel room—with the little black TV right at the foot at the bed—and we'd just sit in there and laugh and talk about good times and how God has shown up for us. We ain't have a dime to our name, but we enjoyed one another.

All the while, Truly Original still wanted to film. That became tricky. We couldn't tell them, "No, you can't film in my mom's house anymore," especially after winning the battle of the master bedroom.

So we improvised, telling them we'd film at an open-air restaurant or something like that. Anytime they asked to come over and film, we had an excuse.

"Can we film at your mom's house?"

"Sorry, we're renovating and it'll be too noisy this week."

"Can we come over today? Let's get you and your mom sitting down in the kitchen, talking about what happened last week."

"I'm so sorry; they're in here painting and blasting music."

I mean, we'd use any excuse to film anywhere else while we figured out our living situation. And thankfully, the five-figure check that we were all waiting for to get a new place came through from Bravo.

We didn't have time to dwell on anything. We didn't have time to mourn or be sad about where we had landed or how far we had fallen.

I couldn't call the Realtor fast enough, asking him to locate me a stately home in St. Marlo, a gated country-club neighborhood in Duluth, Georgia. I knew I was asking for trouble by demanding he get me a large home, with—and I'll keep it real with you—a moderate credit score, but I refused to go backward. I'm not too proud to say that when the homeowners were approving my lease, I had to be upfront with them and tell them I was going through a divorce, so my credit was shaky, but I could afford this house. I even had to pull out my Bravo contract to prove to them that I was a risk worth taking. Plus I knew that if I got a lot of house, I'd hustle hard to keep it and I never lost it.

It'd be the first of many risks I'd take as a divorcée. It couldn't fail because I didn't have any other choice.

When you're in survival mode, carrying not only the weight of your success but your family's as well, you just have to make it happen. You can't worry about what happens if it doesn't work out or if you're ridiculed in the process. All you're worried about is keeping the roof over your head when you go to sleep at night. That's all I cared about and I was willing to do whatever it took to make it happen for myself and my family.

Finally having my own home felt like such a sweet victory, but the one I celebrated the most was being able to find peace again within my own four walls.

CHAPTER NINE

"She's down for the count! She's down for the count! Five! Four! Three! Two! One!" my brother screamed to a small crowd of kids, all watching me get my ass beat.

I must have been only ten years old at the time, so I had never been in a fight before. I had never wanted to be in a fight before, and here my brother was egging on the bout. Instead of sticking up for me or protecting me like I thought he would've, Hosea was screaming at the top of his lungs, being the damn referee.

The streetlights were about to come on in our neighborhood and we were all about to scatter home, but this girl—whose name I can't remember, probably for my sanity—claimed I hit her. We were all in the middle of a basketball game and although I knew it was a non-contact sport, sometimes you had to throw your weight around on the court. But now this girl was taking things too far.

"Let me go! Let me go!" I screamed with my eyes closed tight, trying to swing my arms as hard as I could to get this girl off me.

I swung and missed. I swung another time and landed on something, but my little fist slipped off as quickly as it landed so it didn't make enough of an impact to slow her down. I opened my eyes to see her focused on me. As she ran toward me, I braced for impact and felt my body collapse to the ground. She had my ponytail—my hair was really long back then—inside her clenched first. My face burned, but everywhere else on my body felt numb.

"No!" the girl screamed back, refusing to let my slight of hitting her slide—although I honestly don't think I hit her at all and if I did it was definitely by accident. Next thing I knew, I felt her entire body weight sit on top of me while I lay on the ground. My chest felt like it was about to give up and give out.

"Ooooh! I think she's down! She's out! It's a TKO!" my brother narrated for the growing crowd, who were ducking down and around him to see the final moments of the match. Thank God cell phones weren't really a thing back then because if this later trended on social media…I mean, I'd honestly have no words.

As the streetlights flickered on, quietly sounding the alarm for all of us to head back home, I stood up, wiped myself off, and hurried off home. I couldn't wait to tell on my brother and tell my mom what he let happen to me.

As soon as we walked through the door, my mother took one look at me and wanted an explanation. With my body still throbbing, and my mind not moving fast enough, my brother answered for me: "She got beat up down the street."

"You got beat up?!" my mom said with concern.

I told my mom the truth—that Hosea stood by and watched as

some girl beat my ass. I got ready to watch my mom get my brother together for not protecting his baby sister, but instead she had the nerve to say:

"How you gon' let that girl beat you up? You should've beat her ass!"

I was stopped in my tracks. It was bad enough I had to take a beating, but now it felt like I was getting another beating all over again—and from my own momma! But even though my face looked shocked, she didn't stop there.

"You stay out from down there if you're gon' get beat up," she warned me. "Don't you be walking around getting beat up by nobody."

And my momma was right. It didn't matter if my brother or my friends from 'round the way were there. At the end of the day, I needed to stand up for myself and protect myself. Clearly, nobody else was going to do it for me so I needed to learn how to do it myself.

Although I got my ass beat that day, I also learned an invaluable lesson I'd take with me throughout my entire life: If I'm ever in a fight, I ain't gon' be the one getting beat up.

* * *

Before Bravo asked me to return for a second season, I could've sworn my first reunion on *Real Housewives* was going to be my last one, so I honestly just wanted to get the day over with. I didn't have a husband anymore; why would they keep me?

It was a crisp morning that day in late March when a car picked me up from my house, headed for the Atlanta Biltmore Hotel, where I'd film the reunion for twelve hours straight.

I showed up empty. I literally had nothing to give. I was going through a divorce. I was depressed. I was barely eating, barely sleeping. I had lost so much weight; when we filmed I was only 145 pounds. I was so skinny.

By the time the season had ended, Kordell had stopped filming and I would have to sneak the camera crew into my house to film confessionals. He'd leave and go to the golf course and I'd call and say, "Okay, y'all can come now." It was a whole mess.

So trying to convince Kordell to show up to the reunion was a lost cause. I tried to convince him anyway, only for him to tell me, "I'm not going. You can have that show."

All season long I had had to deal with the ladies questioning my marriage, questioning my desire to be submissive, and questioning just about everything about Kordell. It felt like I was walking into a battleground without any armor. I had to deal with Kordell, once again, not being a man of his word and supporting me.

I thought that filming the reunion—the one time during the entire season that all the ladies sat down with executive producer and host Andy Cohen to talk about everything that happened—was going to be fun. Before I joined the franchise, I imagined I'd be serving looks while serving shade on the couch, getting everybody together for the shade they threw during confessionals, but in reality, I was terrified.

This was before cast members would coordinate a color to wear on the reunion couches, so I picked this floor-length black gown for what I thought was going to be my last-ever filming for *Real Housewives*.

Every *Housewives* show has its own unique relationship with Andy, other executive producers, the in-the-field producers, your castmates, their husbands and children. But because I got thrown into filming without much support or a playbook on how to film a reality show, I made so many mistakes. I really had to learn the hard way.

When I first joined in season five, I didn't realize that producers on the ground were steadily listening to you, learning about little things happening in your life and trying to decide if that tidbit fit the show's narrative or the story they're trying to craft for you that season. I didn't realize it was part of their job description.

After spending hours, days, weeks, and months with producers, you become friendly with them. Look at my costar Kandi Burruss: She even married one of our producers. So you definitely get close, but if you're a newbie, you might mistake producers on set for your friends, and they're not. So now, you're running your mouth about things you honestly didn't intend to let millions of people into and are then forced to put it on the show. Now I know better. Now I know not to share any more than I want to show.

I also got really used to having uncomfortable conversations on camera. If cameras weren't following my life, I'd have a disagreement with a friend and maybe avoid it until I'd cooled down or may just avoid it forever, sweep it under the rug.

Well, on reality TV you have to face everything. If I go to lunch and I say something and one of my friends repeats it, producers aren't going to ignore the fact that I should feel some type of way because my friend repeated something I told her in confidence, so now I have to confront her. It makes you face conflict and deal with issues you wouldn't deal with normally.

It definitely makes it more difficult to form long-lasting friendships because you're always dealing with conflict. Many of the girls will just have an alliance instead, because who wants to be the odd housewife out on the reunion couch trying to defend herself? Nobody.

By the time I sat down on that bright-neon-green couch at the reunion, I was ready to defend the person I truly was and the woman whom fans had yet to meet. I wasn't a kept housewife. I was an entrepreneur who gave up everything because she fell in love.

So I let everybody have it. I had enough of being poked and prodded about the choices I had made in my life and in my marriage. Just as I had suspected, Kordell was targeted for not being a supportive husband and for being controlling. While he might have been all those things and even more behind closed doors, on that couch I still protected him. I protected us. I protected our family.

I let it all out. I preached a four-minute sermon, saying I was still a wife, trying to figure it out. "I'm not perfect. Kordell is not perfect by far, but he's my husband," I said on that couch. I was real. I was authentic and I wasn't going to be shut up and dismissed. Then, in true churchy fashion, I finished it off with a rendition of "Amazing Grace."

I was authentic and transparent that day, and that's what made Andy say, "Keep Porsha's entire four-minute speech in the reunion, and let's have her back on the show for another season."

If my first reunion taping was about finding myself, my second reunion taping was about losing myself.

By the time I sat on a very different couch during our season six reunion, I had been accused of cheating on Kordell, and it did not sit well with me at all because the number one thing I prided myself on during our very volatile marriage was that I never cheated on him; never thought about another man; never looked at another man.

In my marriage, I really tried to be the biblical wife. I really tried to model my life the way the Bible said a wife needed to be. Even when Kordell and I were having hard times, and we'd have many hard times, I would pray for him. Even when I couldn't stand him, I would hold on to the promise I made to him and to God at that altar.

In my mind, we didn't have a marriage. We had a covenant with God, so I felt it was my duty and my purpose to be a good wife and use that to please God. It was completely tied to my spirituality. It was my way of praising God and thanking Him for giving me the gift of a husband and a protector, after so many years of disappointment.

When it came to my marriage, barely anyone knew what we were actually going through. I knew there were certain parts of my marriage that I covered up. During my entire first season on *Housewives*, I put a mask on and tried to pretend we were perfect and we just weren't. But the one thing that was true and real was my loyalty and my faith.

I came out of character at that reunion, and it regretfully taught me to never give my power to a bully again.

Although I'll always regret what happened and how she triggered me to step all the way out of my character, it also revealed to me the power of authenticity.

I paid a price for that decision at the reunion. I was served with an arrest warrant, charged with misdemeanor battery, and even had to take a mug shot—the most fabulous mug shot you've ever seen, thank you very much.

More important, the audience saw a very real breakdown. I lost my peach the next season and received a pay cut, but I didn't let that stop me from being transparent in front of the cameras. I struggled in front of millions of people—but because I allowed them to see that I was a real woman, capable of making impulsive decisions, the audience didn't turn on me, they fell in love with me.

I made a choice right then: It didn't matter what Porsha I was at the time—fed up and frustrated or flourishing and fulfilled—I'd always keep it real about my pursuit to be my best self.

CHAPTER TEN

After my divorce, I didn't need anything from men. Nothing.

I didn't need their love. I didn't need their attention. I didn't need their time. I didn't need their gifts. I didn't need them to tell me who I was to value who I was. I didn't need them at all. It was the first time in my entire life when I felt that I was truly enough all by myself.

I just wanted men to love me. Perhaps it had something to do with my father passing away at the exact age I started noticing men, and their affections, that left me in such longing for affection. It was almost like at the very moment I needed him to show me the ropes, teach me how to duck, or swing, or get back in the ring, or tap out, he left me. Through no fault of his own, he left me here to figure it out when I had no clue how to figure it out. So I played it by ear. I did what men told me to do. I sacrificed every little piece of me if it meant building up pieces of them.

I didn't realize then what I know now, which is that love—in every form—begins with yourself. You've got to know your worth, your value, your dreams, your ambition, what drives you, and what motivates you in order for you to properly love anybody else. And I have that and more now.

For years I asked God, "Why would you tell me Kordell was my husband only for it to blow up in my face? Why would you put me through that?" It took me years to actually hear His answer.

Because I'm His child, God wanted to give me every single thing I wanted—even if it was outside of His will. I desperately wanted Kordell to be my husband, so God wanted to provide, but it didn't mean that was His intention for my life. So what happens when you step outside God's will? He moves closer to you, making sure that even as you move in uncharted territory you're still covered by His grace. It was truly the grace of God that kept me alive during that marriage, I've learned.

After I grew into a woman who knew exactly what she wanted, I never encountered another abusive relationship again. If I'm being honest, I still don't know what shift happened to break that cycle in my life, but if I had to distill it down into one finite idea it would be that I had finally grown into my power.

And not only that, I grew into my purpose.

I had people I used to watch on television as a child, people I had looked up to, people I had admired, now stopping me in the street, telling me that they were rooting for me.

I'll never forget the time that I was flying back to Atlanta from Los Angeles after doing a photo shoot with my crew from *Dish Nation*: Rickey Smiley, Da Brat, Gary with da Tea, and Headkrack. We were all in first class when I got up to go to the bathroom. That's when I heard a very distinct and familiar voice say, "Porsha! Porsha!"

I turned my head to see Samuel L. Jackson.

Inside, I was freaking out because (duh!) this was Samuel L. Jackson, but I tried to play it as cool as possible. He was talking to Headkrack about something I couldn't hear over the plane's hum, but I pretended to be in on whatever joke they were laughing at.

"Oh hey, what's up, Samuel?" I said, absolutely thrilled to speak with one of my idols.

"Yeah, you just keep doing what you're doing. I watch y'all, man. Y'all doing y'all thing."

It was such a brief encounter, but it was also an amazing reminder to keep my head down and keep doing the work. Sam—I feel like I can call him that now since we're friends. Ha!—reminded me that I'm doing the work and now I'm on the radar. People that I've admired forever, they see me. They see what I'm doing. They respect me. It's just another level of validation that I'm doing a good job.

And let me be clear, my power or purpose had nothing to do with celebrity run-ins. It's not about having money, or status, or fame. It had nothing to do with my grandfather or being on *The Real Housewives of Atlanta*. Instead, it had everything to do with knowing who I am.

Another amazing outcome after my divorce was the growth of my empire.

I took the nothing that I was left with and turned it into something. I went from being insecure in my relationship to being an investor in multiple businesses.

I only endorsed brands that I believed in, and that's one of the reasons my companies are successful—because when I'm speaking about them, I'm speaking about them from a place of truth. I have to have some sort of an emotional attachment.

Go Naked Hair, my luxury hair extension company that I founded with my sister in 2013, truly came out of my divorce. I noticed that whenever I looked beautiful, I felt beautiful. At that time, I would do anything to lift me from the very hurtful fog of letting go. So I started expressing myself through my hair by choosing different looks.

Nostalgia also plays a huge part in choosing what companies I work with and get excited about. One of the reasons I started Pampered by Porsha, luxurious sheets that are affordable and will transform any bed into an oasis, was because my mom put these same sheets on my bed without me knowing, and I fell in love with them.

I know it sounds crazy, but I've always loved buying sheets for my bed. My obsession came from the same place as most good things in my life—my mom, who would always be in the store buying sheets when I was a kid. Not to mention, I have always loved lying in my momma's bed. That was part of my childhood. It was my comfort place. She would always let me be in her room with her. Her sheets always felt like butter across my skin. If I'm ever at my momma's house, even today, and I want to take a nap in her bed, I know it will be the best sleep of my life. It's her smell, her perfume, her comforting jersey and cotton sheets; they just remind me of my mom.

Before I go into any company or business deal, I pray about it and sleep on it. Once I trust in the vision and I feel confident about it and I've done the due diligence to ensure it's the right move for me, there's nothing that can stand in my way to make it happen. If obstacles sprout up with starting the business, those are just things I need to work through, because I know it'll come to pass. I just believe in the vision that much.

I get that from my mother, too—my unwavering belief in myself. In business, my mom could be up against insurmountable odds but because God told her that it would come to pass, it would end up manifesting. The act of stepping out on faith was embedded in my spirit after I watched my mom practice her faith and understanding that faith without works was dead. That the very act of moving, whether or not you understand what God has in store, is what activates your faith.

My mom may not have had all the resources—whether that was due to bad credit, debt, or inexperienced business partners—but she taught me that if you have faith it'll come to pass.

She speaks life into everything that she does. She silences out any critic saying what she can't do. I saw this when she was opening her twenty-four-hour daycare center. I remember someone questioning her like, "What makes you think you can pull this off? No one has ever done this before in the state of Georgia." And I'll never forget her response: "Why not me?"

I appreciate that my mom elevated me through the lessons she learned from falling then picking herself back up. I'm better because of her transparency. My mom took her faults in business and was transparent about them so that I could win. When she took a couple of hits from working with friends, it taught me to ensure I have a solid team around me to build my brand. My manager Karen helped facilitate and manifest my businesses. And now that I have money to invest, my accountant and financial advisers help me build my legacy because at this point, I'm no longer working for me. I'm working for my daughter, I'm working for future generations. It's what my mother did for me and so I have to pass that down.

Along with growing my business, I was now open to growing in my dating life again, too. I was now exercising my power of discernment.

I couldn't date just any ol' body because I now had a lot to lose. I'd finally created standards for myself and if the men in my life couldn't live up to them, I was more than willing to text them goodbye.

I was finally making rules in my relationships. I was the girl who now said, "Listen, don't post me on social media. I don't want people to know we're talking until it's serious." If they didn't take my boundaries seriously, I'd stop dating them. Period.

After not having many standards at all, finally finding them felt like freedom to me. Being able to say goodbye, or don't call me again, simply because they did not meet the expectations I had for love and partnership, was freeing.

It was also restrictive at times if I'm being honest. Whereas before my feelings could lead me astray and sweep me to shore with the tide, my new standards kept me anchored yet guarded.

It didn't help that at the same time, I was starting to make choices for *Real Housewives* that ended up deeply shaping my personal life. I often felt that to play my part on the show, I had to show off who I was dating. It's something I feel only happens with certain housewives. On other franchises, if the women got divorced, I didn't see them dragging who they were dating onto the show. But for me, it felt like I needed to have a man in my life—on the show.

It not only led me to choosing men I wouldn't have necessarily dated, but also forced me to hide relationships with men that I cared for. There was one man I dated off and on for years, but because he didn't want to film, it essentially broke us up. I called him my Mr. Big, à la *Sex and the City*. He was just a really great guy whom I had traveled with and spent holidays with, but because of what I did for a living and because of his own situations, we could never get our timing right. So I began dating other people on the show, and no respectable man is going to watch his woman date someone else on TV.

I told men, "If you don't want to film, then I'm sorry, you need to sit over there and wait till I finish filming and then I'll get back to you. If you can't fit in my life, then get the hell out of here." If you didn't want to date me when I had the time to date you, then I said goodbye.

But leave it to God to whisper in my ear yet again, rub me on my back, and gently remind me that everyone, including men, deserved grace. Everyone, including men, deserved second chances. I couldn't just construct a life and then pluck a man and place him in a house that I had bought or make him sign a contract to have a baby.

I told God, *All right, fine. Clearly, my strategy isn't working for my personal life so I'll just chill. I'll wait until you send him. But God, at least let us have chemistry.*

And when I first met Dennis McKinley, we had fire chemistry.

It was actually after taping a reunion for *Real Housewives* when I bumped into McKinley. That's what my stylist, Jeremy Haynes, called him—using his last name—when he first told me about this hand-some bachelor who owned a couple of clubs in Atlanta. When Jeremy said, "Let's go to the club," after filming the reunion for fourteen hours straight, I said, "Eff it, why not? I just finished arguing with these women for hours. Let's go get drunk."

It didn't matter that I had on a black Adidas tracksuit because I refused to be uncomfortable for a second longer. At least I was in full hair and makeup.

By the time that Jeremy, Lauren, my makeup artist, and my assistant-turned-friend, Dom, walked into Dream, we were looking for a good time.

When we first walked into Dream, it kind of looked like a fairy tale. Everything looked really whimsical. There were clouds and over-sized mushrooms on the walls. It looked like we had just stepped into a gentleman's club built by Willy Wonka.

I was drinking away the fact that every other girl in there was dressed up looking cute while I was in a tracksuit when Jeremy told me that we were about to meet the owner. I wasn't paying too much attention, though; I've met plenty of club owners doing bookings over the years. So I shook Dennis's hand and kept it moving. It hadn't yet clicked that this was the same "McKinley" Jeremy had just told me about.

After a couple of hours of dancing to bass-heavy music in dimmed lights, I was getting sleepy. Having been at the reunion all day, I was ready to go. But when I stepped outside I had a boot on my car. *What the hell! A boot?* I wasn't parked illegally or in a crazy spot or anything. It didn't make any sense to me. Jeremy ran back in the club, saying he'd get McKinley to come and get "this boot off your car."

(Later on, I found out that Dennis had put the boot on my car so I'd have an excuse to talk to him later that night. He literally called the city so he could be the superman and get the boot taken off.)

Sure enough, that night Dennis came out there saying, "Aww, I'll take care of it. I got you. I got you."

It was kind of genius. It showed me that Dennis was willing to get creative in order to get to know me a little bit better.

From that night, when he also purposely slipped his number into my friend's phone so I could call him later, it took about three months of playing phone tag and a couple of late-night calls until we actually went out.

When Dennis walked into McCormick & Schmick's, a lovely seafood restaurant in Atlanta, I barely even recognized him because when we'd met at his nightclub, which he eventually shut down to open several other businesses, I was sleepy, tipsy, and ready to go home after seeing a boot on my car. So when our eyes finally met in the restaurant, I was taken aback…in a good way. He was handsome. He had these really warm eyes and a great smile. Just looking at him made me light up.

At that first dinner, we spoke about everything. We spoke about being entrepreneurs and how we both started off running businesses in the hair industry, which I didn't realize we had in common. That was when Dennis dropped a little bomb on me.

"You know, our first time meeting each other wasn't at the club."

"It wasn't?"

"Nah, we met at Bronner Bros. Yeah, it must've been like four years ago," he said, smoothly. "I guess you thought I was trying to holla at you so you kinda brushed me off."

"Oh yeah. Then that was me. That sounds like me."

I was at Bronner Bros. International Beauty Show, the largest exhibition for Black hair care professionals in the country held every year in Atlanta, promoting Go Naked Hair, which was only a couple of years old at that point. Meanwhile, Dennis was there with Queen Virgin Remy, a hair care company he later sold. It's funny because the work boundaries I began on the sets of those music videos back in my early twenties are the same work boundaries I had decades later. I hated mixing business and pleasure. In that moment, though, I was just glad my boundaries still made space to meet again.

At dinner, Dennis and I couldn't stop talking because we realized we were so much alike. We connected over being close with our moms and working with our moms. I didn't think about any of the things you're not supposed to ask on first dates; I went straight for the tough questions.

"Do you have any kids?"

"No, but I want kids one day with the right person. Do you have any kids?" he shot back with a smile.

"No, but I do want kids."

Since we're the same age, I was a little shocked that he didn't have kids yet, but for some reason it comforted me. I guess it put us on an even playing field...except for when it came to marriages. I told him I was divorced and that I starred on *The Real Housewives of Atlanta*.

"Do you watch it?"

"Nah, I don't really watch that show, but of course I'm familiar."

From our very first in-depth conversation, Dennis felt so sincere and genuine. It's why I was enamored of him from the very beginning. I could tell he was truthful. Nothing felt hidden when I spoke to Dennis, and it meant a lot to me that he could say what he wanted without pretense. Dennis was also very sure of what he wanted, and he wanted a lot out of life—to be successful, to have a family, to have love. Although we were still getting to know each other, I wanted that for him, too.

After dinner, Dennis invited me back to his industrial-style condo. I was blown away because the vibe he had created inside his home was very cool. It taught me so much about the man I had just had a fabulous dinner with. Dennis had beautiful artwork on every inch of the wall. Here I thought he was this regular dude, but he was actually very cultured.

We watched *Family Feud* all night, laughing, drinking, and trying to guess which family would go home with the prize money. Next thing I noticed, Dennis was typing furiously on his phone.

"Porsha, I've gotta go to my club real quick to handle something."

I felt my heart sink because I didn't want our day to end. But if anybody understood the sacrifices you made for your businesses, it was me. So I tried not to let the disappointment show on my face.

"Oh, okay," I said a little too casually.

"No, you don't have to leave. Stay right here and I'll be right, right back," he said, showing me that he was on the same wavelength.

By the time Dennis had closed the door, I was hype. What is it about men leaving you in their place that makes you feel like you're

The One? Because that's exactly how I felt. After the good food, the good drinks, and the good conversation, I was so gassed up by the time he left me inside his condo. I felt so special, and it had been a long time since I felt that way.

By the time he got back, I had already pictured myself hanging in one of those frames on the walls, becoming a true part of this man's life and his house.

Dennis reminded me of my father in so many unspoken ways. In the ways I could verbalize: Dennis was a businessman, my father was a businessman. I felt secure and safe around Dennis, and I felt secure and safe around my father. I also loved that he had a dominant nature about him because I'm a boss in my day-to-day life so to have someone else make decisions felt like a breath of fresh air. I definitely look to my partner to have that audacity to know what's best for his life and, at times, for mine.

After handling whatever he needed to handle at Dream, Dennis was now back on his couch beside me. By this time in the evening, Dennis had leaned over and placed his head in my lap. With his eyes piercing through his thick-rimmed glasses, Dennis said, "I love you."

I didn't say a word, but my face must have registered my shock so Dennis said, "I do. I'll show you. I love you."

So now I'm thinking, *Okay dude. You're either drunk or crazy.*

"No, I'm not messing around," he said, reading my mind.

"Okay, Dennis. I'll remind you in the morning that you said this."

* * *

"Hee hee, hoooo! Hee hee, hoooo!"

It was March 22, my daughter Pilar Jhena's birthday, and I was clutching my stomach breathing heavily through my teeth. My duffel bag for my stay at North Fulton Hospital was in the trunk, along with another bag full of Pilar's first miniature outfit changes.

I was blessed to be able to pick my daughter's birthday. Because I live with fibroids, I knew that giving birth to PJ meant I'd be welcoming her into this world thanks to a scheduled cesarean section. Although I struggled with the thought of not having a natural birth like every other woman in my family, it also gave me an unexpected blessing: I got to hand-select my daughter's birthday. March 22 meant that PJ would follow in the footsteps of me, her mother, who was born on June 22, and her grandmother, who was brought into this world on January 22.

"Hee hee, hoooo! Hee hee, hoooo! Hurry! Hurry!" I pushed out through fits of giggles.

Dennis or my sister was behind the wheel, I can't remember which one now, but I do remember pretending like I had labored breathing as we sped toward the hospital. We weren't speeding because we needed to get there for me—even if I was breathing through my teeth as I saw plenty of mothers do on TV while fighting through contractions—but because we were running late. I just wanted to experience what it might've been like if I was actually having contractions, but of course there was no reason to panic because Pilar's birth was ordained.

The night before my daughter's birthday, she was up like it was the night before Christmas. She kept bumping around in there, almost like she knew the very next morning was a big day for her. But thankfully she eventually settled down and cozied up inside me one last time.

It was actually the first time in weeks that I didn't feel any pain so I slept a few hours that night. Nobody really tells you what pregnancy is like—mothers probably keep that information close to the chest on purpose because if they told women the real deal they'd probably think twice—but I had been suffering with pelvic pain for weeks as Pilar grew bigger and bigger, crushing the fibroids that had grown right along with her. But the night before her birthday, that pain had somehow disappeared.

During the nine months that I carried Pilar, my daughter and I became extremely close.

The food that the chef was cooking wafted upstairs, and it smelled soooo goooood, but because I was only hours away from major surgery me and Baby PJ couldn't have any. Instead, music was playing in my bedroom, creating the vibes as I tried my best to get ready to meet my daughter. I had my makeup artist give me a look that would last for hours, honey, and laid my edges down with some tight curls.

Downstairs the rest of my family, including Dennis, my mom, his mom, and my sister Lauren were having a party. They were having brunch, popping bottles, and cameras were documenting the day for my spin-off show, *Porsha's Having a Baby*, which followed my journey of pregnancy and motherhood. It was like the best birthday party ever.

I had already called off filming the baby special once before, right when I hit my third trimester and my body and my mind were solely focused on growing this tiny little miracle baby. Once the third trimester hit, so did the pain of what my body was going through. After I'd suffered a miscarriage due to my fibroids, here they were again making this pregnancy physically hard.

I was still living with fibroids that had begun to degenerate because PJ was outgrowing them and taking their hormones and everything else they needed to grow for herself. Go girl! And while I was thrilled that my miracle baby was growing bigger and bigger, it also meant I was experiencing the painful deterioration of these fibroids. I landed in the hospital for about a week just to deal with the pain; that's how painful it is when they start to degenerate.

So here I was coming off bedrest and telling Bravo and Truly Original, the same production company that films *Real Housewives*, that I just couldn't do this. It was too much. I was irritated. I just wanted to lie down and be ugly all day while eating the house downnnn. I didn't want to be all glammed up in hair and makeup, sitting in front of confessionals sharing about this very high-risk pregnancy and telling too much about my relationship.

But Truly promised to make it easy. They promised to stay out of the way and capture all the big moments in PJ's life like her baby shower and her birth. But of course it ended up being wayyy more than that: my relationship with Dennis, where we were going to live, were we getting married, was I gonna be a baby momma, were our mothers going to get along? But before I realized all of that, once I started feeling better, I agreed to let them create a special where PJ could look back on one day and see just how much she was loved before she even stepped foot on this earth.

As the GoPro cameras attached to the windshield of my car captured us, I walked into this smaller hospital in Roswell, Georgia, to welcome my daughter into this world. North Fulton was such a small hospital that the producers couldn't believe I was giving birth there. But my doctor was the chief of staff at this hospital and I liked the fact that it felt like a family when I walked through the door; I mean, I knew the nurses by name.

If I couldn't be home to deliver PJ, which was my ultimate dream, this intimate space was the best alternative. Living with fibroids had stolen a lot from me and it literally stole my dream of having an at-home birth inside my bathtub, which was hard for me to deal with. If I had it my way, I'd be at home with Dennis and a doula intimately welcoming PJ naturally.

But after having my myomectomy, where doctors had to remove the little tumors growing inside me, doctors told me that I'd never be able to give birth naturally. For a woman in her thirties, hearing that you'll never be able to give birth the "normal way" is devastating. What kind of woman can't give birth? Would my partner still love me if I couldn't give birth naturally to our children? Would my future children be okay?

The pressure we put on ourselves as women is too damn much, but these were real questions that swirled around in my head when I first heard that news. It felt like my womanhood was straight taken from me.

To be told you have to have a C-section when you've never even pictured yourself having a C-section—it was hard to wrap my mind around the idea of having surgery instead of loving pushes to welcome PJ.

It was hard to believe that this was my reality when my sister had a vaginal birth, my mother had a vaginal birth, and my grandmother had a vaginal birth. In fact, I didn't even know anyone in my family who'd had a C-section.

Although time has a way of easing every single fear, it also makes you anxious. And because I was having my daughter later in life, I wanted to experience every single facet of pregnancy and childbirth. I put so much pressure on myself because I had waited so long for this moment and I wanted life to deliver what it had promised me.

But I put the feelings of disappointment of not being able to have a natural birth to the side because I was just happy to be pregnant, being that I had lived through a miscarriage before due to my fibroids. I was just thankful that this baby had been strong enough and had grown big enough to outgrow them. Like the foremothers before her, PJ saved her own life. She's a fighter, clearly. So I had to rest in the feeling of gratefulness for being able to usher her into this world however and whenever.

Since the cameras were capturing my every move, I made sure to have Coco and Chanel—that's what I call my girls—sitting up looking nice in my green bodycon dress paired with a flowy duster. Listen, I might've been nine months' pregnant but my booty was still looking good from the back. From that angle, you couldn't even tell I was pregnant.

I was floating on my daughter's birthday, enjoying every single solitary moment—taking pictures in front of the hospital with my family, teasing our moms who were about to become grandmothers at any second, and enjoying those last few moments before we got to meet her.

I didn't get anxious about giving birth until right before my surgery, when I had to wash my entire body down with this red dye to completely sanitize myself. When I heard, "Take off your dress and go wash yourself with this," it finally hit me that they were about to operate.

I remember turning on the shower, freaking out. As the water washed over me and my bulging baby bump, I just remembered thinking, *Oh my God, I'm washing myself because they're about to cut me open and take this baby out!* As I took the red dye and covered my body with it, I remembered seeing my hands shaking. I was petrified. What if the epidural didn't work and I spent the rest of my life in pain anytime it rained? What if something went wrong with PJ? What if something went wrong with me? I couldn't stop those "what if" thoughts from pouring into my mind. It was all about to happen. I just had to have faith that it would be okay.

Everybody—my mom, Dennis's mom, my sister, my stepmom Lisa, my assistant—was in my hospital room because I had a suite. I knew I couldn't walk back into the room freaking out because it would freak everybody else out.

Okay, Porsha. Okay, girl. Get it together, okay? Okay! You got this, I said to myself, trying very hard to convince myself to calm down before I walked back into the room and lay down on the hospital bed, which was actually more comfortable than you'd imagine. But I couldn't speak. I didn't say another word because I was just paralyzed with fear.

It didn't take long for my surgery to begin. Dennis must've walked in at the wrong time because his face turned white. He looked like he had just seen a ghost when he walked into the operating room, well after they had already started the C-section. Meanwhile, the epidural thankfully was performed expertly by the hospital so I didn't feel a thing.

"You're going to feel some tugging," my doctor said, snapping me back to the reality that I'd be meeting my daughter in mere seconds.

I felt my body vibrate and push and pull and push and pull. I had to just let my body flail on the table since my arms were strapped down beside me—typical for a C-section.

As they gently grabbed her and pulled her out into this world, taking her from the safety of the world she created inside me, I began to cry. *Oh my God*, I just remembered thinking, *this is happening. I'm going to meet her. I'm going to meet this little person I've gotten to know so intimately.*

While I carried Pilar, while I prepared Pilar for this world, I got to know her every move. I knew her moods even while she was inside me: I knew when she was excited. I knew when she was calm. I knew when she fell asleep. I knew when she was wide awake. I knew when she was happy. I knew when she was scared because she would often mimic me.

If I was nervous and upset, she would tightly ball herself up, nestling right underneath my ribs, almost as if she was holding on to them. So I would have to calm myself down because I knew that she could feel her mother was upset. And even before she came into this world, I was teaching her that she was the only person who could bring ultimate peace into her life and who could control her emotions instead of letting them get the best of her—a lesson that I had to learn the hard way.

The tears started falling on my face harder once I heard Pilar's gentle cry, singing in unison. *Waaah! Waaah! Waaah!* Pilar sang, her voice sounding like angelic church bells, marking her arrival.

Pilar's tears set off a familial domino effect because I started crying, Dennis started crying, and then my mom was crying. We welcomed her into this world with wide eyes and the happiest of tears.

When the nurses brought her over to me, I remember saying, "Look at this baby! This is crazy!" They laid her on my chest, ensuring that necessary skin-to-skin contact so she knew and understood that I was her mother before being passed around to other protectors—like her father, because I was adamant about Dennis giving her a bath— and others who'd make her first hours of life just a bit easier for her. It was just magical.

My daughter saved my life.

I've dealt with depression on and off my entire life. I've never been clinically diagnosed, but I know what depression looks like. I know what it feels like. It's almost like a wave drifting on the shore; I can see it out near the horizon, steadily coming toward me until it overtakes me and I have no choice but to give in to it. I've even had one or two times in my life where it felt like my feet were stuck in the sand when it happened and I didn't want to be here anymore, letting it wash me away into the deep.

But I always knew that if I ever had a child, I'd want to live for her. Because no matter how bad things got, no matter how stressed I felt, no matter how low I hung, no matter how closed in my circumstances made me feel, no matter how far my feet sank into the quickening sand, I would always want to fight to be better for her. I'd always want to seek the stronger Porsha for her. I'd always want to be better for her, and work on my mental health for her, and take time for me, for her.

I always knew that my daughter would allow me to treat myself better—and be more patient with myself and forgiving with myself— so that I would be able to mentally be the best mommy. Because she is the light within me, I always knew that once she was here nothing would get so bad that I would ever reach those dark places again.

And I was right. I thank God that ever since I looked into Pilar's eyes, I have not thought about suicide once.

It had more to do with the fact that motherhood was part of my purpose than the actual act of being a mother. Because let's face it, motherhood is fucking hard. It's tough. I realized this in the hospital. Everything was fine during the day, when my family was there and the nurses were coming in and out to check on me and Pilar, but when the sun set and everybody left, and it was just me and her, I knew then I'd never sleep soundly again.

I mean, I was obsessed. My eyes kept darting over to her little bassinet, watching her chest go up and down to make sure she was breathing. It was like staring at my heart. She was, and still is, my literal heart and I had never felt that type of love before in my entire life.

I didn't sleep again…not until Pilar was about three months old.

But when you love someone as much as I love PJ, all those sacrifices you make, like not sleeping, losing your hairline, and trying to breastfeed, all seem minuscule.

She's a part of my purpose. I was always supposed to be a mom. I was just never in a relationship with the right person or it was never the right time. And I remember it used to frustrate me to the point that I ached for motherhood, simply because I knew how fulfilling it would be. I yearned for it—even to the point of thinking selfishly that if I had a child then I could have someone to love me unconditionally.

But after torture, patience grants you clarity. I'm so thankful that God made me an older mommy. I'm thankful that God made me wait and choose the appointed time to enter into motherhood because when I did walk those sacred footsteps that my foremothers carved out, I was completely ready to be a parent. I was responsible, I had a support system, and I had the sheer determination it takes to be a selfless mother.

By the time I gave birth to PJ, I deserved her because I had worked on me enough. I had forgiven myself enough. I had learned who I was enough. I had stopped beating myself down enough to give birth and, more importantly, to give life to another woman. I was more of a complete person.

Even when I gave birth to her and I suffered from postpartum depression, triggered because I was having trouble breastfeeding, I knew there was a light at the end of the tunnel because she was, and still is, that light.

Postpartum depression was unlike any other depression I've ever had in my life because it didn't act the same and it didn't feel the same. I didn't understand why I was low. I didn't understand why I was sad. I didn't really understand why I didn't want to get out of bed or why I didn't want to move. Those were just some very low moments and I eventually chalked it up to my hormones being completely unbalanced after giving birth.

It didn't help that around three months after we welcomed PJ into the world, my relationship with Dennis had started to crumble. So it was just really, really bad. I was so irritated and disappointed with Dennis that I didn't even want to look at him on Instagram so I unfollowed him. Of course, the blogs picked up that I had clicked that button—I don't even know how they keep track of stuff like that—so now my breakup was being turned into internet fodder.

Still, Dennis came into my life for a reason. I knew that he would be the type of father I wanted PJ to have. I knew he would be very loving and very, very, very protective over her. If I was destined to have Pilar as my daughter, it couldn't have happened without Dennis. He was meant to be her dad.

I wanted her to have a dad that was a friend that she could kick it with and not just dictate to her. I wanted a father who was respectful of her feelings and her heart. I wanted somebody who was going to be truthful with her, especially when it came to men. A dad who wouldn't sugarcoat anything, especially the hard moments in life. These are all the things that I would've wanted and I could sense all of this from Dennis while dating him. So I was really comfortable and excited when I found out I was pregnant.

Now that we simply have a friendship, I've come to terms with the fact that he's here to be her dad but not necessarily my husband. Dennis may not have proven himself to be the best partner for me, but he did give me the most amazing gift ever in this world so he'll always be my family.

PJ is our life. She's my life. I see a better day when I look at her. There's nothing that I can't accomplish because I look at her and understand she's my driving force.

Thankfully, my mother was living with me at the time, helping me keep my head above water. She helped with the household chores and with Pilar so my baby was always taken care of. She also gave me sacred space and a little bit of time to focus on myself. Thanks to her holding some of the load, I was able to strengthen my mind and myself for baby PJ. She reminded me to reach for my faith and trust in God to make me the strongest mother for my daughter. I fought my way through it. I literally clawed, scratched, and dragged my way through it because I had to.

Thank God for divine mothering and the generational love that sustains.

CHAPTER ELEVEN

I heard Tupac's voice blast through speakers, piercing the negative energy and collective grief that hung in the air like Atlanta's humidity. I couldn't see through the crowd, but it seemed like the protestors gathered around Centennial Olympic Park in downtown Atlanta levitated a bit as he rapped, "I see no changes."

Wearing no makeup, my face mask, and a blue shirt emblazoned with Nipsey Hussle's face on it, another shirt tied around my waist, the most comfortable tennis shoes I could find, two pairs of black pants, and a band over my head, I marched to the Georgia State Capitol, minutes away. We protested for hours on the very first day in June, fighting for police across the country to actually do their jobs and serve the people they were sworn in to protect instead of killing them.

"Show this," Dennis said, referring to how excited everyone was, dancing to the music with their hands in the air. "The media is showing so much negativity on the news, so show this instead."

So I decided to start streaming live from Instagram to my more than six million followers so they could see exactly what was happening on the ground.

It was exactly a week from the day when my heart broke, watching George Floyd's life being violently taken away from him by a soulless police officer who held his knee on this father's neck.

I had seen a lot of police brutality in my lifetime, from family stories to watching the evening news. I had even experienced police brutality, when a police officer became extra aggressive for no reason when asking for my license and registration. He ended up taking my arm, swinging it behind me so hard that I winced in pain. Out of nowhere, he continued to manhandle me before arresting me. And before you ask, yes, I was cooperating.

Still, for some reason watching George Floyd cry desperately for nearly nine minutes for someone to care about his life without one police officer heeding that call, it broke something open inside me; a push from my ancestors that the work still isn't done.

George Floyd's murder lit something ablaze in me when he called out for his mother, a mother who was no longer even in this world. And having just given birth to PJ a little over a year earlier, I felt that mother's pain. And to just watch that police officer treat his life as if George Floyd wasn't somebody's son, as if he wasn't somebody's father, was looking into the eyes of pure evil; a generational evil that needs to be pulled out from the root, stomped out into the ground, buried into a dust-filled decay.

It woke up a birthright inside of me. I've always had a heart for my people. My father raised me to care about my community. My grandfather showed me what it meant to love on community through service and charity. After he marched alongside Dr. Martin Luther King Jr. during the Civil Rights Movement, he brought me with him to marches in Atlanta.

I was only six years old when I attended my first march for civil rights. I was giddy and excited to be doing the work with my grandfather, this man I'd had heard so much about. I had heard how much he had done. I was just happy to be standing alongside him, seeing it happen with my little eyes.

But it wasn't long before we noted the Ku Klux Klan protesting our protest. It was the first time I heard the word "nigger" being thrown at me. It was the first time I was attacked with rocks. It was the first time we were chased all the way back to old yellow school buses that had brought us to the protest to fight for a better life here.

And the worst part about it was some of the windows were rolled down in that bus and so as the KKK continued to throw rocks at us, some of them were landing on the hard dark-green leather. A few brave protestors had to duck as they boarded the buses to roll the windows up before the rest of us filed on.

On that very first day in June, and the fourth night of protests in Atlanta, I was reminded of that time that I had experienced racism for the first time and just how unnerving it can be.

I'm Black, living in America, so I know what racism looks like, I know what it smells like, and I even know when it tries to hide. I've been ignored while shopping when I have good money to spend in my pocket, knowing that the sales associates' eyes are glazing over me because of the color of my skin. I've been in jewelry stores and have been told about their financing plan before I've even opened my mouth, or directed to a cheaper case because they thought "I'd like these instead." I've been called a nigger and have been flipped the bird, simply for switching lanes in traffic.

Even when I lived in my condo, having the penthouse unit didn't stop me from experiencing microaggressions and racism from the neighbors. I remember it was my first week in the building and I was taking my dog out for a walk. We exited the elevator when I spotted my neighbor. She looked at me with warm eyes and began to speak. I thought she was welcoming me to the building when all of a sudden she opened her mouth and asked, "Are you the dog walker?"

I couldn't believe it. I honestly couldn't believe it. Here I was, thinking I'd moved on up, living in my penthouse unit in downtown Atlanta, and I was still getting mistaken for the friggin' dog walker. And there's nothing wrong with being a dog walker. Hell, I did that job for free for my little pooch, but you know what I mean.

I told that woman: "No, I live here. That's my unit…that I pay for!"

She didn't even look that embarrassed before she sauntered off down the hallway. And I wish she was the only ignorant person living in that building, but she wasn't. Along with being called the dog walker, I also was mistaken for the nanny. It felt like they were trying to continuously remind me that I wasn't supposed to be in that building; that somehow I wasn't good enough to be there and if I was there, it must be because I was in service to someone else who had the means. It was psychological, manipulative warfare.

That's how racism works. It's oftentimes quiet. It's subtle. It makes you believe that you're the one who's crazy and not the person who's perpetrating the ignorance. It makes you question yourself. It makes you feel uncomfortable. It makes you feel isolated and ashamed and exhausted. And after a while, it makes you want to give it up altogether, and stop trying, just so you don't have to deal with it anymore.

After hearing the music bumping through the speakers, I and a few protestors noticed that there weren't just local police officers patrolling the protest. The National Guard troops—holding their clear riot shields and wearing goggles, gas masks, army fatigues, and helmets that were more appropriate on a battlefield than downtown Atlanta—had showed up, trying to intimidate us. They started to take a knee, which we know former NFL quarterback Colin Kaepernick turned into a symbol of fighting police brutality on the sidelines of his games. We were all so happy, like *Oh my God, they're taking a knee. They're with us. They get it. They understand that we're not protesting them, we're protesting the brutality that they, as an institution, have inflicted upon us.*

Then those officers, down on their knees, pulled on their gas masks. It didn't take me long to figure out that what they'd do next wouldn't be peaceful, even though we were peacefully protesting, which is a constitutional right.

All of a sudden we heard what sounded like gunshots ring out all around us, vibrating the ground we protested on. They were so powerful it felt like our insides were vibrating, too. If you know anything about Black people in a crowd, you know we run first and ask questions later. All I heard was, "Oh, shit!" and "They shooting!" and Dennis and I just took off running.

"It's gas! It's gas! Go, go, go, go, go," I yelled at the dozens of pro-testors all around me as one tear gas canister flew right by my head, missing it by inches. I instinctually watched the round canisters fall to the ground, bursting.

I knew what a gunshot sounded like since I own several guns, and that wasn't the sound of a bullet. Instead, after watching so many pro-tests on TV, I recognized the tear gas canisters police were now throwing into the crowd, trying to disperse us for no good reason. And I knew we could jump over them and dodge them if we just kept running.

"Run, baby!" I yelled at Dennis, trying to make sure we didn't get split up in the mayhem.

The two of us were weaving through the streets about to get hit by cars that were trying to escape the intersection while we jumped over tear gas bombs, with many still flying past our heads. But it wasn't before long that the gas started hitting us and I ran right into that poisonous smoke.

"My eyes!" I yelled at no one in particular when I realized the gas had smacked me right in my face.

I closed my eyes immediately to relieve the pain, but it still felt like my eyes were burning from the inside out. They were burning with a devilish sensation that I had never felt before. It felt like they had exploded in my head. I could hardly catch my breath.

It wasn't until someone physically stopped me, screaming they had an "anti-tear-gas" solution and milk, that I stopped running. I tried to open my eyes, but the pain kept closing them shut. I wanted to see what they had for me, what they held in their hands to make sure I wasn't running into another trap set by the police, but it felt like I couldn't. I'd just have to trust. They grabbed me by the arms and told me to kneel down a bit and lean forward.

"Open your eyes. Open your eyes," the nameless protestor instructed in that moment of deep torture. I decided to trust a stranger and do as he said. Although they were burning, my eyes were still working and allowed me to see that this man was holding a gallon of milk.

"Don't rub your face, okay?" this ally said. "Just tilt your head back."

I held my breath as the cool milk poured down my face and into my eyes just a little bit to relieve them. It didn't stop them from burning completely, but it definitely helped.

While I was literally running for my life—just like I ran for my life when I was peacefully protesting at six years old—I never stopped recording. They tried to silence us in that moment, not realizing that technology allowed us to yell from the mountaintops that our own National Guard was being turned on us to strip away one of our civil liberties.

My chanting was replaced with fits of coughs as the poison ran through my system. Although he was coughing, too, Dennis asked me if I was okay.

"I'm good. I'm good," I pushed out, trying to stop myself from coughing without any luck just yet.

"Do y'all see this?" I said while catching my breath, staring right at that tiny camera inside my phone. "We're in Atlanta. It's seven forty-five. The curfew is not until nine o'clock. We're out here peacefully protesting and they tear-gassed us for no reason at all."

To stay off the streets and out of the waves of tear gas that hung in the air, I crouched down in the underbelly of a downtown Atlanta office building. It was the same office building I had driven past a million times on my way to work and on my way home. It felt odd that in this moment, it felt like a fort in a war zone.

In fact, in a matter of months it seemed like all of America had been turned into a minefield of emotional and physical torture. I had made up my mind that I wasn't ever going to protest again, to be honest, because I was hurt. I was let down. I felt like my home had turned on me.

I'm born and raised in Atlanta. It's a place where I was so proud to embody and represent. In Atlanta, I felt a real sense of community and family.

But after that protest, I didn't recognize the city that made me. To literally run for my life in the middle of downtown Atlanta streets, trying to avoid cars as they barreled down the familiar roads, was traumatizing, to say the least. I felt like I was at war in my own home.

It didn't help when I discovered that my cousin and his girlfriend were assaulted by the police. His girlfriend's jaw was broken and everything. This place couldn't be my city; a city my family and I had poured so much of ourselves into to make better. It couldn't. I looked into the eyes of the people sworn in to protect us and simply saw rage. I looked into the eyes of the men and women who were there to hold up our democracy and all I saw were cold riot shields.

I thought to myself, *This is dangerous. This is too dangerous. I have a daughter. What am I even doing? What am I doing out here?*

Protesting with hundreds of my neighbors made me ask the

ultimate question to laser-focus my mission: What am I doing to be most effective to meet this moment? Because the reality is I didn't want to go out on the front lines again, get hurt, and then not be there for my daughter, Pilar, for my own family, for my own community. And so I really took time to investigate what my personal goals were in running to the front lines and then figuring out how to pull it off in a way that made the most sense to me.

It's what I encourage every person who's down for the cause of bettering Black lives around the world to do for themselves. Everyone can't be on the front lines, and to be quite honest, we don't need everyone on the front lines. There is an activism ecosystem and every person, no matter their race or ethnicity, has their place. For some that might mean protesting on the front lines; for others it might be making protest first-aid kits to hand out to protestors in need; for another group of conscious citizens it might mean donating money for bail funds so that protestors aren't sitting in dirty jail cells while fighting for the right to peacefully protest. And for an entirely different group of people, it might be cold-calling our government representatives, demanding action.

So I had to ask myself, what am I doing to be most effective? To answer that question for myself, I had to do the hard work of pushing past my emotions and my anger and my frustration as a Black woman, continually disappointed with America, to really ask what I wanted. I wanted to scream and show my outrage, hurt, anger, and pain to let the government know that killing unarmed Black people was not okay. Having a lack of accountability in our police systems was not okay and we're not going to stand for it.

But when I took it a step further, I discovered that my whole reason for going out to protest on the front lines was not only to be in community with my neighbors, but also to help elevate the voices that are continually silenced through systematic exclusion or societal convenience. I knew I had this platform and I knew the power it held to elevate. I wanted to use that power for good.

I wanted to remind myself and fellow Americans that I am George Floyd. I am Sandra Bland. I am Tanisha Anderson. I am Natasha McKenna. I am Yvette Smith. I am Miriam Carey. I am Rekia Boyd. I am Breonna Taylor.

I am a Black woman. I have a brother. I have a daughter. I have a family. And we're all fighting for our humanity; for our humanity to be recognized when we're speaking, when we're driving, when we're jogging, when we're sleeping in our beds in our own homes, when we're laughing, when we're listening to music really loudly in our cars because that's the best way to listen to it, when we're going to the store for candy and juice, when we're outside with our friends. I wanted George Floyd's family and all of the other people taken from this life at the hands of police to know that they did not die in vain.

After wading through the waters of my emotions, I finally realized what I demanded from my government: I want the US government to end police brutality and to end qualified immunity or a doctrine that makes it hard for citizens to hold government officials accountable for their misconduct and malpractice.

Although I had figured out what I expected from my government, it still felt very discouraging because it felt like they weren't listening. We'd been out in the streets protesting in Atlanta for weeks and it didn't feel like enough had been done that felt close to restorative justice.

So I tried to fill this burning feeling in my soul that searched for justice: I did interviews so people knew and intimately understood what was happening to peaceful protestors in the streets. I wanted people to know that Black people were in the streets fighting and wanting to be heard and now we were fighting to be able to fight peacefully.

By the time I had heard about Breonna Taylor's disturbing story, where this twenty-six-year-old Black woman was shot and killed by police while lying in her bed, I was on fire. There was already a heavy cloud on the entire world, and when I learned her case's details, it became unbearable. It was just heartbreaking. I could not believe that this had happened in America and that no one had been arrested for the crime. I was burning in my bones. Oh my God, even thinking about it to this day makes me fill up with purposeful rage.

As a Black woman, it felt as if I now had a bounty on my head. It made me feel under attack in my own home. As soon as I heard her story, how police were executing a no-knock drug warrant due to a botched investigation that had nothing to do with Breonna or her boyfriend, Kenneth Walker, I immediately placed myself in her situation. When police barreled through their door, her boyfriend shot at them, thinking they were intruders. Although an officer was hit, police fired back, killing Breonna. Her boyfriend, thankfully, wasn't hit.

I placed my mother, my sister, my daughter in her shoes. Breonna seemed like an everyday Black girl, someone that I would hang with, someone I knew, someone in my family. Her story was just too relatable to me. It hit home.

Bringing Breonna Taylor's family justice felt like something that needed to be handled immediately and I felt pulled to do everything that I could to help raise awareness of who this woman was and how her life was violently and carelessly taken away from her.

What upset me even more was the lack of media coverage Breonna Taylor's case was getting; it almost felt like another injustice, as if she was being systematically silenced. This is a Black woman killed in her own home by the police's negligence. Where was the outcry?

The reason media coverage matters is because you've got to get the government's attention. The government needs to know that we're outraged, this is not okay, and all eyes are on you to do the right thing. We needed to galvanize the public to force the government into doing its job; one that seems overwhelmingly hard to do when it comes to Black bodies.

I knew that I had at least six million people I could share Breonna Taylor's story with, so I started posting on social media. But that didn't feel like enough. I started calling the Kentucky Attorney General's office to tell Daniel Cameron that I wanted justice for Breonna Taylor. But the number was always busy and I could never get through, I couldn't reach him. So that didn't feel enough.

I started searching online forums about police brutality, trying to come up with a strategy where I could personally be effective. I wanted to figure out which officials I should really be concentrating on to ensure they knew we wanted justice for Breonna. I started following activists in the Black Lives Matter movement and beyond so I could stay best informed about what was happening on the ground.

It was during that strategy session that the name Tamika Mallory bubbled to the top of my mind. I had heard of this magnetic woman who was speaking and teaching and raising her voice for Black lives, and for some reason I just thought: Let me go to her Instagram page and see what she's talking about. It just so happened she was posting about Breonna Taylor. In fact, one of her last posts was promoting a direct-action protest in Kentucky in honor of her. I immediately DM'd her.

Mind you, at this point I didn't even know what a direct-action protest was. I knew that it was a protest, but I didn't know what kind of protest. I didn't really care, though. I just felt this incredible pull to do more and to be there.

In a flurry from my fingertips I wrote, "Hi, I'm Porsha Williams. I want to get more information about this protest you're having this weekend."

By the time I had sent the direct message, I saw that she had already messaged me, reaching out after seeing me being politically active. Still, Tamika replied, "Hi Porsha, so glad to hear from you."

She gave me the time. She gave me the date and then she wrote, "And we're going to meet here. Prepare to be arrested by 3 o'clock."

I read that and I thought to myself, *Don't threaten me with a good time*. I had been looking to do more to help the situation, elevate this tragedy, and bring a shining light to Breonna Taylor's case, and if I could do something radical like this, and force people to pay attention, I was going to do it—by any means necessary.

THE PURSUIT OF PORSHA

That's when I decided to look up the definition of a direct-action protest and discovered that it's when a group of protestors intentionally break the law to get arrested, which eventually leads to some sort of change happening. It was the "more" that I was looking for. I wanted to be bold and radical to kick-start change in this case. So I immediately DM'd her back.

"I'll be there."

It was the night before the protest, but that didn't matter. Kentucky was only a couple of hours away by plane. So I checked Delta Air Lines, looked up flights, and chose one that flew me right into Louisville, Kentucky, just in time for the protest. Before I bought the ticket, however, I had to call Dennis. He had to go with me.

"Porsha, how are we going to Kentucky? It's literally the night before."

"So!"

"So, I don't think we should go by ourselves. What if we both get arrested? We can't both get arrested."

"Why not? Why shouldn't we both get arrested?" I asked Dennis, not believing what I was hearing. "We'll both get out."

"P, we're both Pilar's parents. We can't both get arrested," Dennis said firmly.

Mind you, none of that had even crossed my mind. When Dennis said Pilar's name, though, instead of it deterring me, it made me want to press my way to Kentucky even more. Because while I could kiss and rock my baby to sleep at night, Tamika Palmer, Breonna's mother, would never ever have that luxury again.

With Dennis thinking a bit more rationally, I tried calling a couple of other friends to head down to Kentucky with me, but they weren't trying to come, especially since it was the night before. "No, I just can't up and go like that," one friend told me. "Girl, I gotta work," another one said. My sister couldn't come because she's a single parent so she said she didn't want to get arrested and have no one there to take care of her daughter at all. I completely understood that, but it didn't deter me. I just felt like: Fine, this is my mission then, this burning desire for justice that had dropped down in my spirit.

I was about to press the button to buy my plane ticket when Dennis called me back and said that he'd go with me. He definitely didn't want me to go to another state to protest alone.

We had decided that we both weren't going to get arrested, for the sake of our child who'd be waiting at home for us with my mom. So I volunteered because I had a platform and I was the one the press would write about. If I got arrested, it would hopefully bring more attention to Breonna Taylor's case because it would be splashed in the headlines the next day that Porsha Williams got arrested at a Breonna Taylor protest. It'd be a sacrifice that I was willing to make.

On the flight to Kentucky, I read Martin Luther King Jr.'s inspiring "Letter from a Birmingham Jail," where he explains how he uses nonviolent resistance and his work with direct action. Reading more about his work encouraged me even more as we made our way to Louisville. We still didn't even know where we were going when we walked off that Delta flight the next day. We didn't know anything. But that was by design. The organizers, a social justice organization called Until Freedom who were hoping to ban no-knock warrants across the state of Kentucky in honor of Breonna Taylor, didn't want infiltrators and agitators to have the ability to disrupt the mission of the protest.

We eventually received word of where we'd be peacefully protesting on that July day: in the St. Matthews area of Louisville. We ended up on the front lawn of Attorney General Daniel Cameron's home with about a hundred other people. No one was being destructive. No one was tearing up his yard. No one was being belligerent. No one was doing anything except for sitting on the ground with our legs and arms crossed, being 100 percent peaceful.

Although I was sitting next to Tamika and Linda Sarsour, one of the co-founders of Until Freedom, I could also see reality star Yandy Smith peacefully protesting along with NFL player Kenny Stills and rapper Cordae.

It wasn't long before police in militarized gear surrounded us. Knowing what happened to Breonna, it was hard to ignore the guns in their holsters. If I didn't feel ready and prepared, it could've been a scary situation. But I had already stepped into my grandfather's legacy.

So many people speak about generational curses, but one thing that doesn't get brought up enough is generational blessings. I truly felt in that moment that I had inherited his power, his courage, his fearlessness, his bravery, his audacity, his hope, his belief in a better outcome for our people. At any point where fear was, I would just think about my grandfather and his life's purpose and how he had to put the cause above his own fear, making deeply personal sacrifices despite what mattered to him at that moment.

Then they began arresting us, one by one. You would think that would be the moment that I would've freaked out or tensed up or gotten scared, but I did none of those things. I was very calm. It felt like I was doing what I meant to do.

I watched as the women before me, who were handcuffed just like I was, were placed into a white police van. Inside the paddy wagon, a bar separated the women from the men, who were both facing the van's walls. After you sat down in the van, you were handcuffed to a bar on the back of each seat and, thankfully—unlike in the death of Freddie Gray—they put your seat belt on. It was just big enough for you to sit down on either side of the van. In fact, there was only an inch between your knee and the van's wall; that's how tight it was in there. It was hot too because, of course, there was no air-conditioning back there, at all.

Thankfully, it wasn't quiet because handcuffed to one of the bars inside the van with me was a preacher who also happened to be an activist. Breaking the thick heat that permeated into that van was his voice singing: "We shall overcoooome. We shall overcoooome. We shall overcome sooooomedaaaaaaaay. Deeeeep in our heartttsssss, Iiiii still beliiiiiieve. We shall overcoooome soooomedaaaay."

Instinctually everyone in that van who knew the words, sewn into our hearts thanks to our foremothers and forefathers, joined him in singing the freedom song. It was a song I remembered singing with my grandfather when we marched back when I was a little girl.

In that moment it really felt like I had embodied him. In that moment it felt like I was back in time, sadly reliving the same struggle. In that moment I saw very clearly a small taste of what he had gone through in 1965 when he led the "Bloody Sunday" march in

Selma, Alabama, where some six hundred marchers were tear-gassed and beaten while trying to march to the state's capital in a fight for voters' rights. I was even more fortunate because I had not been beaten, bloodied, or accosted. At that moment, I just kept thinking, *Wow, here we are decades later and we're in the exact same position they had been in, fighting against the injustices that Black people endure.*

As the police van pulled up to the gate, I watched as policemen and -women unloaded us from the van and began separating us. When we first walked into the jail, all you could see was silver fencing and a completely cemented area. It felt intentionally cold and purposefully uninviting.

Along with the women who were arrested alongside me, I was put into a filthy cage just big enough for one person. Spiderwebs floated in the corners of the cage—the only sign of life in that jail. My hands were handcuffed to the fence for good measure and the police took my mask, which bore the name of Breonna Taylor. They replaced it with their own mask...because, in case you forgot, we were still protesting in the middle of a pandemic; fighting for our lives on every front. The men, however, suffered more in the holding area, because they were configured in some sort of chain gang. All you could hear were the shackles banging up against each other.

For the first time since we had been put in handcuffs, a silence fell over the protestors. It was almost as if we had all realized at the same time that we were standing inside a jail cell. It doesn't matter how prepared you are for that moment, it comes with a sobering humility.

At that point, I got a little scared because they had started separating us and I didn't want to be separated. Sandra Bland's case was still fresh in my mind. She died in police custody in Texas after a state trooper pulled her over for a minor traffic violation, and authorities there couldn't explain it or didn't want to explain it. And here I was, down in Kentucky, being separated from my group. Who knows what they could do to me and get away with? Sandra Bland filmed her traffic stop and she was still found hung in her jail cell. They've already killed plenty of Black women in jail, what made me think I was so different?

Every time they brought in a busload of protestors, the inside of the jail erupted into cheers and claps. By the day's end, eighty-seven people were arrested and charged. I was charged with disorderly conduct, criminal trespassing, and intimidating a participant in a legal process, a felony that carried a sentence of one to five years in prison if convicted. Thankfully, the felony charge for every protestor was dropped after a very long process, but it's still not stricken from my record.

If everything in my life had brought me to this place to be gifted a platform to raise awareness and raise my voice to advocate for my people, then all of it would've been worth it. All of it.

My grandfather laid out a plan to push beyond struggle so I could elevate to purpose. Although I didn't realize it when I was a little girl marching alongside him, I watched. I listened. I took notes. I heard his conviction. I felt his pride; the same pride I felt for my people when I risked my own life on the front lines to yell, scream, and sing that what they're giving us isn't good enough. And it never was.

That little girl who sat in her room staring at the end of black lenses because she felt an emptiness inside her was using those same lenses to broadcast and call attention to the injustices plaguing her people.

As a child, I might have found comfort in those lenses, but as a woman, especially as a Black woman, I found power.

EPILOGUE

Many of these stories contain my pain and my sadness.

I built a very real habit as a child, one where I would dress up my pain so it remained hidden under the makeup, the laughs, and the smiles. While all those smiles were real, I also felt a need to be strong for the people around me. To not make waves. To please the men, the family members, the employees, and the people who looked up to me—to be a perfect version of myself.

But there is no perfect version of me. There's no perfect version of anyone. Now when things in my life hurt, I deal with my pain. I don't dress it up or try to hide it. I ride the waves that life can often bring to shore and try not to worry about pleasing anyone aside myself and my loved ones.

Many of these stories also share my growth, my strength, and my testimony. If these words can help someone find lightness during dark times, then I have accomplished what I set out to do.

I am a work in progress and I always will be. I am still on my journey to becoming the best version of myself, and to finding an even greater happiness than the one I have been blessed with right now.

I am still on my pursuit of Porsha and I hope these words help you in your pursuit, too.

ACKNOWLEDGMENTS

To my family, who have guided me through this journey on my pursuit to Porsha, I wouldn't be here today without your love. Thank you.

Mommy, it's true that a mother knows best. Your wisdom, your compassion, and your dedication to happiness has been my compass directing me to this moment. I am who I am because of you, and you're my world. Thank you for being the best mom to me and the best grandma to PJ. We love you so much.

To my father, grandfather, and grandmother "Big Momma," I love and miss you all. I am determined to keep your legacy alive. xx

Lauren, we've gone through this journey side by side and there is nobody else on the planet I would have chosen as my sister. You've shown me that it is truly incredible what one can accomplish when the people you care about believe in you. You're my therapist and meditation leader and my world. Baleigh, you are so lucky and blessed to have Lauren as your mom. You have the world's greatest role model raising you, and if you follow her lead, you'll see all the beautiful blessings you have to come.

Hosea and Brenton, I am so blessed to have you both as my brothers. I love you so much! Thank you for all you do for our family.

Grandma Iona, I love your witty personality (I think I got some of that!), and your love of family has been the most important lesson for me. You've become a leader for my family, and I love you.

To all my nieces and nephews, I love you so much. Thank you for all the happiness you bring me every day.

Lisa, thank you for being the best stepmom in the world. Your support and love mean so much to me.

Dennis, thank you for being an amazing father to Pilar.

To Karen Kinney, thank you for everything you do. You're more than just my manager...you're my confidante, my visionary, and most importantly, my friend. There aren't enough thank-yous in the world to show my appreciation for you.

To my editorial team, Beth Adams and India Hunter at Hachette, as well as Tess Callero at Europa Content, thank you for giving me the chance to tell my story the way I wanted.

Joi-Marie McKenzie, you gave me the chance to let my deepest thoughts become beautiful words. You made sharing moments I never thought would leave my head into an empowering, uplifting experience, and I'm forever grateful.

Darrell Miller, Eric McGlothen, and Stephen Welch, thank you for being my Watchmen. It means so much to know that y'all always have my back.

Lauren Wilson, thank you for keeping my life in order and my world running.

To Atlanta, I'm a cornbread-fed Georgia Peach for life. This city, this community, and this culture helped me grow up in more ways than one. I'm so blessed I get to be a part of it and that I get to raise my family here.

To my fans, how can I thank you enough? You have rolled with me through all my ups and downs throughout the years and have chosen to support me time and time again. I will never be able to thank you enough for coming on this journey with me. Writing this book and putting myself out here in this way was one of the hardest things I've ever done. I love you all.

And finally, to my daughter, Pilar Jhena. PJ, these stories are for you. May they help you understand where you come from and believe in everything that you can be. You are my life and I'm eternally grateful to God for choosing me to be your mommy. You are my lifesaver, and I will be by your side forever and a day. I love you so much, Pooh bear!

xx

P

ABOUT THE AUTHOR

A true "cornbread-fed Georgia Peach," Porsha Williams was born into a prominent and historic family in Atlanta as the granddaughter of civil rights leader and philanthropist Reverend Hosea Williams. She is deeply committed to various charitable partnerships, including Hosea Helps and March of Dimes, and is active in the ongoing social justice movement.

Porsha's unscripted success includes being a longtime cast member of *The Real Housewives of Atlanta* and star of the highly rated spin-off *Porsha's Having a Baby*, as well as competing on NBC's *The New Celebrity Apprentice*. She currently co-hosts Bravo's late-night talk show *Chat Room* and the nationally syndicated talk show *Dish Nation*, and hosts Stitcher's *Porsha4Real* podcast.

Porsha's scripted projects include costarring alongside Vivica A. Fox and Columbus Short in the theatrical remake of *Two Can Play That Game*, as well as credits in the animated feature *CarGo*, *Sharknado 5: Global Swarming*, HBO's *Insecure*, Fox's *Star*, and TV One's *Steppin' Back to Love*. She is also the executive producer of an upcoming romantic comedy.

A serial entrepreneur, Porsha is the founder of two highly successful, top-ranking businesses, *Pampered By Porsha*, a luxurious yet affordable sheet line, and *Go Naked Hair*, a high-end hair extension and wig company.

Porsha currently resides in Atlanta, Georgia, with her daughter, PJ, and the Williams Family.